Praise for *Imperfect Lead*

The next generation of leaders in education – wheth...
or national organisations – will be so much more successful for reading this readable book which matches theory with fascinating personal stories and cameos. I wish it had been written when I started out as a leader, or later when I was wondering whether or how I could go on as one. Today's leaders can now have it at their side and wise leaders will refer to it on a regular basis.

Sir Tim Brighouse, former London Schools Commissioner and
Chief Education Officer for Birmingham and Oxfordshire

After so many years of us being encouraged to aspire to heroic leadership, Steve Munby's first book *Imperfect Leadership* was a game changer. It showed that anxiety, disappointment and self-doubt aren't weaknesses; they are essential parts of the inner landscape of the most self-aware, humane leaders. This new book with Marie-Claire Bretherton takes those insights to a new level, providing a practical, empowering and uplifting handbook to rejuvenate our own leadership insights and finally kick imposter syndrome into touch.

Geoff Barton, General Secretary, Association of School and College Leaders

In *Imperfect Leadership in Action*, Steve and Marie-Claire offer wise, honest and compelling reflections on leadership. The personal case studies are powerful and persuasive and make the book hard to put down. They share great stories of lives devoted to finding better ways of making more of a difference. All in all, it is an inspiring book but also a very practical one with so many ideas to help refine and improve leadership that it is impossible to close it without learning and aspiring to do better.

Christine Gilbert, Visiting Professor, UCL Institute of Education

Imperfect Leadership in Action should form part of every school leadership team's library. Whether you read it as an individual leader – curious about the notion of imperfect leadership – or as a member of a team wrestling with challenges that we face today, I cannot recommend the book highly enough.

Sir David Carter, former National Schools Commissioner

I predict that any head teacher or senior leader reading this will experience two very powerful emotions. Firstly, a sense of relief that it's okay not to be perfect and to make mistakes. We all talk about being open to self-reflection and learning from our mistakes, but this book makes it so much easier to do. Secondly, a sense of connection or empathy. There is no sugar-coating of the day-to-day realities of leading a school, which means the narrative understands our world and becomes our friend. These two very helpful aspects of the book are combined with a brilliant articulation of what the authors describe as 'the imperfect leadership mindset' – a series of internal and external foundations for successful leadership.

If you want a book that resonates with you, lifts you up and gives you hope and optimism about the future, then look no further. *Imperfect Leadership in Action* is a real gem.

Andy Buck, CEO, Andy Buck Leadership Services, founder of Leadership Matters and creator of the BASIC coaching method

Imperfect Leadership in Action is a book you won't put down. It is a practical, evidence-based guide that is brimming with great leadership advice. Steve Munby and Marie-Claire Bretherton demonstrate wisdom, authority and compassion in every page of this text. This is a must-read for leaders everywhere – it is, quite simply, a tour de force of a book!

Alma Harris, Professor Emeritus, Humanities and Social Sciences Faculty, University of Swansea

Recognising one's imperfections is a hallmark of great leadership, and openness to learning from other people's experience is a condition for any leader's growth. Professor Steve Munby's mantra that 'being an imperfect leader is not a skill set, it is a mindset' is powerfully illustrated in his latest book, co-authored by Marie-Claire Bretherton.

Drawing on the thoughts of a wide range of successful (but self-defined 'imperfect') head teachers and CEOs, they illustrate the dispositions and behaviours that help leaders to be less negatively self-critical in striving to learn from mistakes and become better versions of themselves as they shape organisational culture and foster the self-belief of others.

Readers will be refreshed by the candour, humour and pragmatism of this book, which serves as both a mirror and a route map.

Sir Hamid Patel, CBE, Chief Executive, Star Academies

To produce two books focusing on imperfect leadership seems to be making a point, and there is indeed a message in the title. Steve Munby, joined this time by Marie-Claire Bretherton, builds on his first book and looks at how imperfect leaders manage real situations in schools. Both authors are successful in their field and are held up as examples of excellent practice, so the openness with which they admit to doubts is a powerful message to others that no one gets it all right and that perfection, though often demanded by others, is rarely achieved by anyone.

People will recognise their own leadership successes and dilemmas in the case studies – and this reflection of reality is one of the book's many strengths. We know that there are no easy answers to the many challenges that face school leaders, but too often we don't encourage the skills or allow school leaders the space and time that they need in order to find the best possible solutions. The practical suggestions in this book, together with the examples of others, address this directly and effectively. *Imperfect Leadership in Action* will be a constant and reassuring guide for many in our schools.

Rt Hon Baroness Estelle Morris, former Secretary of State for Education

This book is about the mindset of leadership. It is written with disarming honesty and humility, and is full of integrity. It offers a series of incredibly helpful tools, reflections and ways of thinking which is a little bit of a goldmine for leaders. It does not offer or advocate complacency in imperfection – rather it sees imperfection as a strength and as an opportunity to learn and grow as a leader. In the words allegedly inscribed on Mother Teresa's wall, the book's wisdom is its dictum: 'Give the world the best you have and it may never be enough; Give the world the best you have anyway.'

Leora Cruddas, CBE, Chief Executive Officer, Confederation of School Trusts

Who would have thought that a book called *Imperfect Leadership in Action* would contain countless more ideas about how to be an effective leader than any ten books that promise to make you a great leader? Every one of the eleven chapters can be treated as a stand-alone set of lessons, examples and guiding questions to help you deal with a vexing issue, and to become ever better. Use this book alone and with others and you will be immediately rewarded with ideas, confidence and readiness to act. It is a treasure trove for dealing with the most difficult issues you will face.

Michael Fullan, Professor Emeritus, University of Toronto, and author

Imperfect Leadership in Action is probably the perfect sequel to *Imperfect Leadership*. The latter encourages education leaders to humbly strive to become better leaders, not for perfection, but for service to education. The former, as the title implies, shows these leaders in action. From the pens of Steve and Marie-Claire, this book brings the experiences of imperfect leaders to readers as case studies for learning. In the book, one can find stories of the joys, frustrations, successes and struggles of education leaders in various situations. Readers will probably see some of themselves in these stories – and will gain much from reflecting on and responding to them.

Imperfect Leadership in Action is a wonderful gift to school leaders who would like to reflect on and improve their own leadership in practical ways, encouraged by the understanding that the lonely path of leadership need not be that lonely after all.

Pak Tee Ng, National Institute of Education,
Nanyang Technological University, Singapore

Authenticity, integrity and inspiration are words I have often used when describing Steve Munby. This book is rich in all three. For me, it is *the* book on school leadership – and that is also thanks to the pragmatism, generosity and insight of Steve's co-author Marie-Claire Bretherton.

Richard Gerver, educator, speaker and author

Imperfect Leadership in Action is a remarkably useful and deeply human book. With wisdom and authenticity, Steve Munby and Marie-Claire Bretherton invite leaders into a space of self-discovery, reflection and growth. Every educational leader can benefit from these empowering mindsets, practical frameworks and inspiring examples.

Dr Simon Breakspear, Adjunct Senior Lecturer, Gonski Institute for Education, the
University of New South Wales (UNSW), and author of *Teaching Sprints*

Imperfect Leadership in Action is a refreshingly candid and inspiring reminder of the importance of leadership character, and of the worth of investing in its development through the many reflective activities and exercises that are included. The engaging writing style and rich examples make this book a very worthy follow-up to *Imperfect Leadership*.

Viviane Robinson, Emeritus Distinguished Professor, University of Auckland,
and author of *Reduce Change to Increase Improvement*

Steve Munby and Marie-Claire Bretherton

Imperfect Leadership In Action

A practical book for school leaders who know they don't know it all

Foreword by Andy Hargreaves

Crown House Publishing Limited
www.crownhouse.co.uk

First published by

Crown House Publishing Ltd
Crown Buildings, Bancyfelin, Carmarthen, Wales, SA33 5ND, UK
www.crownhouse.co.uk

and

Crown House Publishing Company LLC
PO Box 2223, Williston, VT 05495, USA
www.crownhousepublishing.com

Page 70: Murphy, D. (2020) 'What Improv, Ubuntu, and Covid-19 have taught me about leadership'. Presidential address to the British Psychological Society Conference [online], September. Available at: https://thepsychologist.bps.org.uk/volume-33/september-2020/what-improv-ubuntu-and-covid-19-have-taught-me-about-leadership. Used with kind permission.

Page 139: The relationship between core values and beliefs and practices, 'From values and beliefs about learning to principles and practice', p. 4. Available at: http://www.learning-by-design.com/papers/From Values & Beliefs to Prin & Prac.pdf © Julia Atkin, 1996. Used with kind permission.

Page 141: Teaching to the North-East © Russell Bishop (2019) *Teaching to the North-East: Relationship-Based Learning in Practice.* Wellington: NZCER Press. Abraham, M. (2020) 'From founding documents to guiding frameworks: innovation at HPSS (Part 2)', Principal Possum (31 January). Available at: http://principalpossum.blogspot.com/2020/01/from-founding-documents-to-guiding_31.html. Used with kind permission.

Page 144: sunflower image © #CHANNELM2 – stock.adobe.com.

Page 168: 'Come to the edge', from *Selected Poems* by Christopher Logue (1969) © Christopher Logue.

Page 222: Phases of recovery from disaster © Zunin and Myers adapted as cited in DeWolfe, D. J. (2000) *Training Manual for Mental Health and Human Service Workers in Major Disasters,* 2nd edn. Washington, DC: US Department of Health and Human Services, Substance Abuse and Mental Health Services Administration, Center for Mental Health Services, p. 5. Used with kind permission.

Page 232: Extract from 'Looking for the Castle, Second Time Around' © William Ayot: From *E-Mail from the Soul: New & Selected Leadership Poems.* Glastonbury: PS Avalon. Used with permission from the author.

British Library of Cataloguing-in-Publication Data
A catalogue entry for this book is available from the British Library.

Print ISBN 978-178583601-5
Mobi ISBN 978-178583614-5
ePub ISBN 978-178583615-2
ePDF ISBN 978-178583616-9

LCCN 2021950840

Printed and bound in the UK by
Charlesworth Press, Wakefield, West Yorkshire

Foreword by Andy Hargreaves

It is pointless to strive to be imperfect. And it is impossible to achieve the opposite of imperfection for long in anything that truly matters. In most areas of life, perfection is a futile goal. Zero tolerance policies, elimination of achievement gaps, the insistence that failure is not an option and impeccable leadership – for most things, in most circumstances, these ends are all unattainable. Not only are they unattainable, they are not even desirable. The cosmetically altered wrinkle-free face, the orthodontically perfect row of teeth, the flawlessly scripted speech – don't all of these lose a vital part of what makes us human, distinct and interesting? As the late Leonard Cohen pointed out, 'There is crack in everything'. And that, he added, is 'where the light gets in'.

Striving for excellence is admirable. Pursuing perfection is a trap. In *Overcoming Perfectionism*, Ann W. Smith (2013, p. 8) argues that 'the desire to be superhuman becomes a problem when we begin to believe that perfection is actually possible and even necessary for self-esteem, success, peace of mind, and acceptance by others'. Relentless perfectionism, she writes, ultimately leads to obsessiveness, depression, addictive behaviour and burnout.

The truth is that we are all imperfect. Whether we are parents, colleagues, performers or leaders, imperfection is something we can never escape. It is part of the human condition. In 'Imperfections', Celine Dion sings about how she has her 'own imperfections', her 'own set of scars to hide'. We need to remember that this applies to children too, sometimes. As every parent knows, it is unrealistic to expect young people to be perfectly behaved all the time.

Being an imperfect leader is not something we can deliberately accomplish, like being a transformational, inspirational or servant leader, for example. Imperfection will happen to us anyway. We cannot avoid it. Imperfect leadership, rather, is about how we handle our imperfections and make the most of them, while eliminating or at least mitigating their harmful effects on others. Imperfect leadership is about acknowledging our own and each other's flaws, learning from them and even loving each other for them a bit – like the brilliant but absent-minded professor, the efficient manager who can get a bit too uptight on occasion, or the passionate yet vulnerable leader whose heart on their sleeve may sometimes beat too loudly for other people's comfort.

The issue that Steve Munby and Marie-Claire Bretherton address in this excellent book is not how to become an imperfect leader on purpose. Trying to come across as a mere mortal when you truly believe you are a hero or a god will only be a source of irritation as well as ineffectiveness. False humility, staged self-deprecation and insincere apologies are as unconvincing as the forced grins that people try to pass off as genuine smiles. They are as excruciating in real life as they are in Ricky Gervais' fictional leadership portrayals in the TV sitcom, *The Office*.

There is a depth of authenticity and honesty, rather than just a level of skill or sophistication, which marks out the imperfect leader as someone we can trust, admire and follow. Imperfect leadership is about who we are and how we are with others, which is manifested in what we do and seek to accomplish with those around us, together. It is not a toolbox or a rule book for leadership that has no connection to the development of our inner selves.

At the same time, imperfect leadership is no excuse for hapless or incompetent leadership. And while public disclosures by sport stars and celebrities about their struggles with mental health have made it easier for everyone to stop covering up their flaws, expressing weakness or vulnerability can be overdone if it degenerates into emotional indulgence. Indeed, in a paper critiquing the rise of psychological interest in well-being as a way of dealing with unresolved issues of social inequality, for example, University of Birmingham professor Kathryn Ecclestone (2011, p. 99) has pointed to how the concept of vulnerability has expanded beyond 'those with mental illness or disability, and those unable to protect themselves from harm and exploitation to anyone receiving any health treatment, therapy or palliative care'. Other categories like post-traumatic stress and depression have also expanded to become more all-encompassing over recent years.

To sum up: imperfection is not a get-out clause for poor performance; vulnerability must not descend into self-obsession; and apologies for mistakes are no substitute for redemption and restitution concerning those we have wronged.

Clearly, when we look at the idea of imperfection, and at the nature of imperfect leadership, there is more to them than meets the eye. In this excellent sequel to *Imperfect Leadership*, Steve Munby – a proven leader of school districts, of an iconic national organisation for educational leadership and of a global education charity – joins forces with Marie-Claire Bretherton – a highly experienced school leader and one of the education system's best collaborators and school improvers – to look more closely at imperfect leadership in action.

Their book identifies some key attributes and actions that characterise imperfect leaders. Some of these, such as the importance of trust, building relationships, admitting mistakes and empowering teams, are already very familiar in the literature of leadership, although it is good to read about them once more from a practical and not just a theoretical standpoint. Other attributes are more novel and may, momentarily, take the reader aback. Making public promises that could come back to haunt you, doing the right thing even when your career prospects are put at risk, narrating compelling stories as well as sharing important data and, my favourite, finding the right balance and relationship between power and love in interactions with others – these are all explained clearly and also illustrated practically from both the authors' own extensive leadership experiences and from inspiring case examples of imperfect school leadership all around the world. There are engaging tools for personal reflection and practical guides for how to manage processes more effectively as a self-avowed imperfect leader. The cases ring true. No blushes are spared. The authentic nature of struggle, setbacks and overcoming adversity leaps off almost every page.

I have known Steve Munby for forty years. When he was a friend and colleague early on in our careers, he always struck me as someone who was simultaneously courageous and terrified all at the same time. He always wanted to make a positive difference, he was sometimes terrified by what he had taken on, and yet, with lots of help and advice, including a bit of my own, he always found a way through in the end. In later years, in some of my most challenging leadership moments, my own dark nights of the soul, I have sought Steve's advice in turn, and benefitted from the moral support, strategic insight and ultimate optimism of his coaching support.

And now we are colleagues together, leading an international organisation that we have created with a small team of associates, which serves seven ministers of education, their senior civil servants and their professional leaders, so we can advance humanitarian goals, policies and strategies in education globally. Through this work, we have been able to help system leaders to be imperfect leaders, too, in how they strive for genuine improvement, work collaboratively with others and admit it when they have taken a wrong turn or feel stuck.

To be an imperfect leader is human. To live imperfect leadership with others can sometimes attain an almost transcendent quality that reaches far beyond the individual ego to encompass something greater than oneself.

This book will change your thinking. If you are worn out with trying to be perfect, it may change your life. Best of all, if you take its lessons seriously, it may help to change the lives of everyone else that you care about as an educator.

Acknowledgements

Both

Together we'd like to thank our trusted friends and colleagues who kindly gave us detailed and helpful feedback on this book in its earliest form. To Maggie Farrar, Geoff Southworth, Peter Batty and Helen Barker – thank you! Your wisdom and insights really helped shape our thinking and our articulation of the imperfect leadership mindset.

We also want to say a heartfelt and huge thank you to our case study writers – we are so grateful that you were willing to open up your leadership to our readers and share your experiences and learning. It's been a privilege to learn from you.

Thanks also to Crown House Publishing who were enthusiastic about the idea of this book from the start and have provided excellent support along the way.

Steve

I made a full list of acknowledgements in my last book so I will be brief in this one. Since I wrote *Imperfect Leadership*, Vanni Treves (formerly chair of the National College for School Leadership) has, sadly, passed away and I would want to acknowledge again what a hugely positive influence he had on my leadership. I would also like to thank Andy Hargreaves not only for his excellent foreword to this book but also for his friendship and unwavering professional support over a 40-year period. Most of all, I want to thank my wife, Jacqui. She was a highly effective (but imperfect) head teacher herself and is now making an equally positive impact as an executive coach of school leaders. She has had more of a positive influence on my leadership than anyone else; providing me with ideas, support and challenge and helping me to believe that I still have something to say on leadership.

Finally, a big thank you to Marie-Claire. Writing with someone else is very different from working solo, and I wasn't sure how it would go. It has been a delight.

Marie-Claire

I am so very grateful for the support, encouragement and kindness of my husband Roger, and my two boys, Leo and Tom, who have graciously allowed me many hours at weekends and in the holidays to read and write. They, along with my dearest friends Joy, Paul, Jude and Jo, have continually championed me and supported me – not just in writing this book, but through many many years of trying to become a better leader, and someone who can make a positive difference to children and young people.

My parents have had a profoundly positive influence on me as a person and as a leader. Both educators, fuelled by a passion to make a difference and to bring people together, and to challenge the status quo in Northern Ireland – they have both been an inspiration to me. I'm so proud of them! I'd like to thank them for giving up hours of their time to proofread an early draft of this book and for the feedback and support throughout.

I would also like to acknowledge my colleagues in Anthem School Trust and in KYRA, some of whom I have known and worked with since I was a new head teacher at Mount Street Academy just finding my feet. I'm so deeply grateful for the support of the community of colleagues around me who help shape me, challenge me, and keep me learning as a leader.

Finally, I want to thank Steve for the opportunity to write this book with him. Spending time talking and thinking about imperfect leadership, and putting our ideas and experiences together on paper, has been hugely rewarding. I'm grateful to him for the concept of imperfect leadership, and the opportunity to share with others the freedom that comes from knowing that no one has all the answers, and no one is a perfect leader.

Contents

Introduction

Marie-Claire

Over a bowl of olives and a glass of wine in a busy London tapas bar, I confessed to my mentor that I had read his book, but that it had disturbed me. As usual, Steve just smiled and said, 'Tell me more.'

Imperfect leadership, as a concept, had blown my mind and turned my view of good leadership on its head. I recall saying something which now seems rather obvious: 'I can be a good leader and still experience failure?' I admitted that my deepest desire to make a difference as a leader, to achieve and be successful, had been built on the notion that to be good at my job, I needed to eradicate or disguise the imperfections in myself and become the perfect leader. That perfect leadership would lead to greater success.

At the time I was facing several big challenges in my leadership and not everything was going well. I was subconsciously telling myself that clearly every success had been a fluke and that now the flaws in my leadership were appearing, like skeletons jumping out of a cupboard I had tried to keep shut.

But there is something powerful and liberating about owning your imperfections as a leader. Being an imperfect leader creates space for learning and growth; it opens up opportunities for others to contribute when we humbly ask for help. It means we can acknowledge mistakes and failures without writing ourselves off. In short, being imperfect as a leader has huge advantages (and the truth is that there is no perfect leader anyway!).

Steve

In *Imperfect Leadership: A Book for Leaders Who Know They Don't Know It All* (Munby, 2019), I outlined my leadership journey over twelve years (from 2005 to 2017) whilst I was CEO of two quite large education organisations: England's National College for School Leadership and the UK-based not-for-profit Education Development Trust. I didn't start off with the title of the book in my mind, but the more I wrote about my leadership, the more I came to understand that 'imperfect' was the best term to describe it. And this is not something I am embarrassed about. I am proud to be an imperfect leader, and I have a problem with the notion of perfect leadership. If we think that we need to be perfect as leaders, we may make ourselves physically or mentally ill. If we think that we need to be perfect as leaders, we won't delegate and distribute leadership to others. If we think that we need to be perfect as leaders, we won't encourage others to step up into leadership because they would need to be seen as being perfect too.

The response to the book was much more positive than I had expected, but I promised myself that I would not write another one, as I had nothing else left to write about. However, I gradually began to think that perhaps the principles of imperfect leadership could be discussed in a way that might be helpful and of practical use to school leaders and aspirant school leaders. But such a book could only work if I could find someone to co-author it with me who understood deeply the principles of imperfect leadership. This person would also need to have a highly successful track record as a head teacher, as well as having experienced ups and downs in leadership and be very close to the real challenges facing school leaders. Marie-Claire was the obvious choice, and it has been a delight to work with her on this book.

What is imperfect leadership?

The book is about imperfect leadership in action. But this is not a book about enacting leadership competencies. We are not asking readers to go through each chapter and tick off whether they meet the criteria. Far from it. We do not want to give the impression that you must strive to be a 'perfect imperfect leader'.

Being an imperfect leader is not a skill set, it is a mindset.

Those with an imperfect leadership mindset understand that self-awareness is the starting point for leadership. They know that it is important to be aware of their strengths and their areas for improvement. They understand that without self-awareness they are unlikely to lead others well, and they won't know how to improve their own leadership.

Those with an imperfect leadership mindset know that they don't know it all, which is why they need a good team around them and why they value the expertise that others bring. It is also why they see it as a wise and positive thing to ask for help rather than something to be ashamed of. Their self-awareness helps them to manage their ego – not too low and not too high – because they know their strengths and their weaknesses. And it is because they are aware of their weaknesses, that they sometimes use public promises to help keep them on track to do the things they know they really ought to do. They never regard themselves as the finished product, so they are always in learning mode.

They understand that they will never be a perfect leader. Instead, they try to be a better version of themselves tomorrow than they were today. And if they have days when that doesn't happen (and there will probably be many of them), they try to be kind to themselves, because they know that perfection is not attainable and if they tried to achieve it, they may damage their health and their sense of self-worth. They don't expect their colleagues who are aspirant leaders to be perfect either. Rather than putting barriers in the way, leaders with an imperfect leadership mindset encourage others to step up into leadership and help to build their confidence. Finally, imperfect leaders are authentic. They know themselves and they see it as important to be honest about who they are.

How to get the most out of this book

This book is built upon, and draws upon, the experience of imperfect leaders. Each chapter is peppered with real examples from leaders around the world who have graciously opened up their own imperfect leadership as case studies to be examined. Every context is different and there is no formula for leadership. Some successful leadership is simply down to luck and to being in the right place at the right time. But the message of this book is that we can all learn to be better leaders if we invest in self-reflection and become skilled at asking for help. The authors of these case studies have done that, with considerable success, even though they may have had some angst along the way. We hope that you will find their stories helpful and inspiring. And where they challenge you, or make you feel uncomfortable, consider what the case study is provoking in you, and take some time to reflect and respond.

Each chapter covers one of the main principles of imperfect leadership outlined in Steve's previous book. Although each principle is discrete, the common theme throughout is that knowing we are imperfect as leaders can be a positive mindset and this can help us to be better and more effective at what we do. Given the unprecedented challenges caused by the COVID-19 pandemic, in Chapter 10 we consider how, as imperfect leaders, we need to show up with hope and pragmatism, particularly in periods of crisis and uncertainty.

Imperfect leaders know themselves well and they are also committed to their own development. So, in each chapter, we have also included some questions for reflection and self-review, and some exercises and activities for you to try out, either on your own or with a trusted colleague or peer. It can be incredibly powerful to have a shared dialogue with others about your leadership learning and reflections. You can make the time to do these exercises and reflect as you progress through each chapter, or revisit them as a way of reviewing and crystallising your thinking.

Embracing the fact that we are imperfect leaders doesn't make us settle for poor performance or mediocrity. In fact, the reverse is the case. Knowing that we are not the finished product makes us keen to learn more, to make better decisions and to improve our leadership. It drives us on, whilst helping us to recognise that some self-doubt can be a good thing. It makes us more ready and willing to ask for help, and it reminds us that we need to lead with love as well as with power. Most of all, it helps us to be authentic and to try, day by day, month by month and year by year, to be a better version of ourselves as leaders. And because we know that we are imperfect, it helps us to still love ourselves when we get it wrong. As the famous poem 'Anyway' ends: 'Give the world the best you have and it may never be enough; Give the world the best you have anyway.'

Key themes

There are a number of key themes in this book, as illustrated below. The imperfect leadership mindset is about being a lifelong student of leadership, working on the internal foundations as well as the external manifestation of our leadership.

The imperfect leadership mindset

3 Asking for Help

2 Developing and Empowering Teams

4 Managing Ego and Acknowledging Mistakes

1 Self-Awareness and Tuning into Context

5 Making Public Promises

7 Power and Love

6 Being a Restless Learner

8 Developing Future Leaders

9 Authenticity and Doing the Right Thing

10 Showing Up with Hope and Pragmatism

Internal foundations ⟵⟶ External manifestation

Chapter 1
Self-Awareness and Tuning into Context

Knowing yourself is the beginning of all wisdom.

Anon.

Imperfect leaders are self-aware – they know their strengths but they are also aware of their weaknesses.

We believe that a deep self-awareness is one of the most important aspects of effective leadership. If leadership is about moving a group of people forwards towards an agreed goal, then the ability of the leaders in the organisation, at every level, to be aware of themselves and their contribution is vital. Self-awareness can help leaders to be more effective by giving them insights into how they might need to reshape actions, reframe conversations and adjust approaches, so they have a better impact. It helps leaders to bring the best of themselves and mitigate for the worst of themselves.

But self-awareness is complex and can be a lifetime's work. There are many things that influence how we behave as leaders: our skills and knowledge, our self-image, our traits, our motives and, of course, external factors and the context in which we are currently. If we want to improve our self-awareness as leaders, we need to ask ourselves a range of questions:

1. What *knowledge, experience* and *skills* do I have that make me an effective leader within my current context? What does my context need from me? What are the gaps?

2.   What do I think *others* want and expect from me as a leader? How do I know? Am I happy with that? Is my self-image as a leader overly influenced by the expectations of others?

3.   How do my *traits* work for or against me as a leader? What are my default modes? When and why do I sometimes end up behaving in a way that I regret afterwards? What am I like when I am tired or stressed? Can I detect the warning signs and amend the negative aspects of my behaviour before harm is done or before I make myself unwell? How might I adapt or change my default modes to make myself more effective?

4.   What *motivates* me about leadership? What are my drivers and how does that affect my behaviour and how I feel about myself? Is my main driver making a difference, status and power, income/paying the mortgage, not being a failure or being liked?

Being an imperfect leader means that you develop an accurate, balanced view of yourself as a leader. You know what you do well, and you know where you have gaps in knowledge, weaknesses or insecurities.

Self-awareness is developed naturally over time through experience and feedback, but there are several ways that self-awareness can be nurtured in a more proactive and deliberate way. We do this through things like:

- Working with a mentor or coach.

- Recording our behaviour in meetings and watching it back, perhaps with a facilitator.

- Inviting external critical friends into our organisation to watch how we operate.

- Keeping a personal diary and using it to reflect on our leadership behaviours and feelings.

Steve

I kept a personal diary for ten years as a leader. It wasn't too onerous, and I only made occasional entries, but it definitely helped me to be more aware of the patterns and habits in my leadership and to reflect on how I was developing on my leadership journey.

One psychological tool that can help to frame how we might expand our self-awareness is the Johari window (see Figure 1.1 on page 10), created by Joseph Luft and Harrington Ingham in 1955. There are two dimensions to the Johari window: what you know or don't know about yourself, and what others know or don't know about you. The model has four quadrants. Firstly, anything you know about yourself and are willing to share is part of your open area (quadrant 1). You can build trust when you disclose information to others, which in turn allows them to share things about themselves as well. However, there will be areas where you have a blind spot (quadrant 2). This is where others around you can see things about you and your leadership of which you are unaware. With the help of feedback from others you can become aware of some of your positive and negative traits, as perceived by others. Clearly, there are also aspects about yourself of which you are aware but might not want others to know. This is known as your hidden area (quadrant 3). This leaves just one area, which is the area that is unknown to you and to others (quadrant 4).

The key is that it is possible to increase your open area by asking for feedback from other people. When feedback is given to you honestly, it can also reduce the size of your blind area. For example, maybe you interrupt people before they have finished speaking, which can cause frustration. Sometimes you don't realise these aspects of your character until it is pointed out to you. By working with others and asking for feedback, it is possible to discover aspects about your leadership that you can build on, develop and improve.

The Johari window reminds us that we all have blind spots or areas where we hide behind a facade. The people around us have a contribution to make to our journey to self-awareness. How we solicit feedback is an important first step in understanding how we are known and perceived by others. (At the end of this chapter there is a simple exercise you can do to begin this process of asking for feedback.)

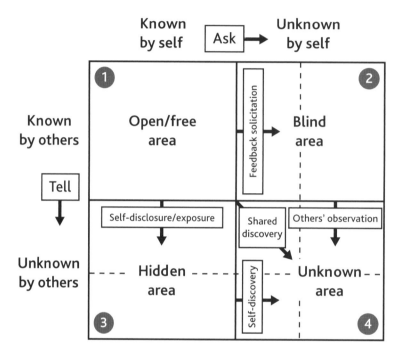

Figure 1.1. The Johari window (Luft and Ingham, 1955)

360° feedback can be a very powerful way of developing self-awareness

The National Professional Qualification for Headship (NPQH) was introduced in England in 1997. This was a part-time programme for prospective head teachers, to be completed over one or two years, leading to a qualification awarded, from 2000 onwards, by the National College for School Leadership on behalf of the government. By 2008, it had become a government requirement that all those applying for their first headship role had to have the qualification or to be enrolled on the programme.

But there was a problem: too many people had achieved the qualification but were either nowhere near ready for headship/principalship or else they didn't really want to become heads. The reputation of the qualification had therefore been diminished; its brand had been tarnished.

One of the changes that was introduced to improve the situation was that all those applying for the NPQH programme were required to take part in a 360°-feedback process. For every applicant, a sample of colleagues would be asked to complete a questionnaire about their leadership. When the applicants received the feedback about their areas of strength and areas for improvement, if they embraced the feedback, recognised it and were keen to work on their weaknesses, they were more likely to be admitted onto the programme. Conversely, if they did not recognise the feedback, challenged it or were overly defensive about their areas for improvement, then they were less likely to be accepted. This was based on the firm belief that self-awareness is a key to effective leadership. Over time, this process worked well as one of the guardians of quality for the development of head teachers.

360° feedback can sometimes challenge us in ways that make us feel uncomfortable or vulnerable. It takes courage and commitment to be open, to listen and reflect; having a balanced attitude is an important foundation. 360° feedback represents other people's perceptions of us, not necessarily the whole truth. Aim to use the feedback as a starting point for more in-depth conversations with a coach or mentor about how you can grow.

Sometimes it is hard for us to accept the positive feedback we get, as too often we fixate on the negative. We have a tendency as humans to overly focus on our weaknesses and deficits rather than be encouraged by the constructive feedback we get. There is an abundance of research about how strengths-based approaches to leadership and personal development have a positive impact on both well-being and performance (Buckingham and Clifton, 2001; Dubreuil et al., 2016). Consider how you can identify and develop further the things you do well as a leader, as well as the areas you want to improve. According to Miglianico et al. (2020), 'The best opportunity for individual development lies in investing in people's strengths, not in managing their weaknesses.' In other words, minimising our weaknesses can prevent failure but it cannot inspire leadership excellence.

There is a risk, of course, that undertaking formal 360° feedback can become just an event or a task on your leadership to-do list. Consider ways in which you can build in frequent micro-moments of feedback from leaders and colleagues in your teams.

Steve

Many years ago, I was a delegate on a four-week full-time leadership programme at INSEAD in Fontainebleau, near Paris. It was a programme mainly for CEOs of private companies. It felt strange to be there and also a privilege. I was used to annual 360° feedback processes at the National College for School Leadership (it was a requirement for all staff), but one of the highlights of the INSEAD programmes for me was a thorough 360° feedback process involving a wide range of colleagues, and also a separate 360° feedback process to elicit feedback about me from my friends and family. That really made me think deeply about my behaviours and default modes. It built up my confidence about my strengths as a leader, but also highlighted my default modes and personal well-being issues. The process unsettled and challenged me. It helped me to think more radically and more proactively about my own well-being and effectiveness as a leader.

For example, the feedback told me that I often came across to my friends and family as overly tired. Some of them questioned whether I needed to review how I was managing my time. In conversations with my tutor at INSEAD, this led to two very important changes in how I prioritised aspects of my work and personal life. For a year or so, I had been feeling guilty that I was not spending as much time as I ought to with my elderly mother who lived 150 miles away. The feedback and reflection process helped me to focus less on the quantity of time I spent with her and more on the quality of that time – on what we did together and how to make it special. This had a very positive impact on my own mental well-being and also, I believe, on my mother's mental well-being.

One of the biggest changes as a result of my experience at INSEAD in general and the 360° feedback in particular was that I decided I should stop working on Sundays. This was a very big decision for me, having worked for most of the day each Sunday for thirty years – ever since I started teaching – and, in my view, very high risk. How would I keep on top of things if I didn't work on Sundays? How could I still be an effective leader without putting in all those extra hours at a weekend? I am writing this during a global pandemic when, in many parts of the world, school principals are under huge pressure and are having to respond to urgent but shifting demands that are beyond their control. I am only too conscious that during this time many school principals have not only been working on Sundays but throughout the school holidays too. So, it is important to emphasise that sometimes a broad well-being principle can be overtaken by extreme circumstances. As far as my own leadership is concerned, apart from a few occasions when I was dealing with urgent crises and apart from the first year of my CEO role at CfBT, I no longer worked much on Sundays for the following nine years.

Leaders need to make their own decisions about well-being and balance based on their own context and awareness of their default modes. But for me, on the whole, I was a better and more effective leader by having Sundays off. Overall, I was less tired and I was able to achieve a better balance between my personal life and my professional life.

We can also develop self-awareness through collaborative or personal self-reflection. Some leadership teams use four questions to help them reflect and become more self-aware as leaders. The questions are based on a model originally developed by the United States Army called an after-action review. An after-action review can be used to analyse what happened, why it happened and how it can be done better. This structured approach can be used to debrief on an action the team has taken or a difficult conversation one member of the team has had with another member of staff. They can also be used to support self-reflection.

The four questions are asked in sequence, allowing the leader to tell the story. The rest of the team listen and ask questions. It is a no-blame conversation and should be free of judgement; the aim is to be curious. (Having a team member take notes is helpful too.) The questions are:

1. What were you trying to do?

2. What actually happened?

3. Why were there differences?

4. What can you learn from this?

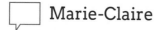 Marie-Claire

One example where an after-action review helped to build my own self-awareness as a leader was when I used these four questions to self-reflect on a difficult interaction I had with a colleague.

What was I trying to do?

Following a Department for Education announcement about changes to school openings during 2020, I thought it would be helpful to send an email containing a list of all the questions that I thought were still unanswered to my colleague who was leading on our communication to schools. My aim was to be helpful and to get the ball rolling. I was trying to offer my support in navigating yet more (sometimes conflicting) information, right at the point when school holidays were beginning and I knew school leaders would be asking for answers.

What actually happened?

I sent my email but it was not well received at all. My colleague rang me and made me aware that the email had been less than helpful and almost tipped her over the edge. She confessed that she was drowning in information and emails, feeling completely overwhelmed and had several other urgent priorities land on her desk that morning (of which I was unaware). I listened to her and apologised, trying to explain what I was trying to do.

Why were there differences?

The reason there were differences between my well-intentioned email and the impact it had on my colleague was a gap in my own self-awareness. On reflection, I was also feeling overwhelmed by the latest information and changes. My response was to jump in and try to make sense of all the details, sending off an email to 'prove' to my colleague (and myself) that I was a good leader and on top of it all. I let my own need to be seen to be competent cloud my judgement about how best to help my colleague.

What can you learn from this?

It would have been much more helpful for me to ring my colleague and have a conversation with her about how we were both feeling in response to the latest information. I could have empathised with her and offered my help from a place of shared responsibility and shared ownership. I am grateful that my colleague picked the phone up to me straight away; although it was a difficult conversation, it helped me to rethink my actions and reflect on my true motivations and drivers.

 Prompts for personal reflection

- How often do you ask a colleague for specific feedback?

- What is the piece of feedback you get most consistently? Why do you think this is?

- What is the most positive feedback you have had about your leadership and how can you build on that?

- Which piece of feedback do you tend to want to ignore and why?

- What feedback would you like to get from your colleagues?

- Consider asking your friends and family for feedback too.

- What more might you do to work with your team to model self-awareness and self-reflection?

- What is it like being on the receiving end of me?

Imperfect leaders tune into their context and adapt their leadership accordingly

Being self-aware is a good foundation for effective leadership, but being aware of your context – and how that context changes over time – is also critical. Self-awareness and context-awareness are both iterative processes and are developed incrementally. Gradually, we cultivate our own personal leadership style. Inevitably, we will be greatly influenced by our own experience and especially by those leaders we work for and with.

 Note

Many years ago, the National College for School Leadership conducted a survey asking leaders about the main influences in their decision to become a head teacher. Overwhelmingly, the most common answer was 'a head teacher I had worked with'. When asked to expand upon this, it turned out that they were referring either to a really impressive head teacher who had inspired them, coached them, believed in them, encouraged them and modelled effective leadership or, alternatively, a very unimpressive head teacher who had made them determined to become a head teacher and do it better!

Our personal leadership style will be based on our experience; our knowledge and expertise; our beliefs, values and aspirations; our personality; and our context or environment. Some of this is fixed but much of it can change – and as a result we may need to alter the way we lead. When it comes to the context or environment, unfortunately, it is not always easy to spot how that might be shifting around us. If we move into a new job or organisation, the situation is obviously different. However, a change in the context around us, when we are in the same job and the same organisation, can be much more subtle and harder to identify. For example, we may find that things that worked for us as leaders last year, even within the same organisation, won't necessarily work for us this year. When the situation around us changes, it may require a new approach from us, but there is a risk that we are so close to things that we don't see the shift until it is too late.

In the insightful case study that follows, Marc Belli analyses how his own leadership style shifted as his context gradually changed over the first two years of his executive leadership role. And, interestingly, he is now wondering whether his leadership approach needs to change again, as the stage of the pandemic shifts.

 ## Case study

Marc Belli, executive head teacher, The Bishop of Llandaff Church in Wales School/ Caldicot School Partnership, Wales

The opportunity to enter into a formal partnership, leading two schools as executive head teacher, came somewhat out of the blue. Unlike in England, executive leadership in Wales was relatively unheard of. Luckily, I had been a head teacher for around ten years and The Bishop of Llandaff Church in Wales School in Cardiff, where I had been head teacher for five years, was in a strong place and I was fortunate to be part of a fantastic leadership team.

Caldicot School in Monmouthshire had always achieved relatively well in relation to its context, but it was in a significant period of transition. Their long-standing head teacher had retired and the school had been unsuccessful in appointing a suitable replacement. 2018 was a particularly difficult year for the school, with a poor set of examination results coupled with a disappointing school inspection. This created a period of uncertainty and, from an external perspective, potential freefall, so, when the invitation came, understandably I was somewhat hesitant.

Reflecting on the first two years of the partnership, I think of the change process in three phases. The first phase was about understanding the context of the school and introducing solutions to the immediate challenges. It would be fair to say that during this phase, my style of leadership was more top-down, offering centrally driven messages which required urgent action. Prior to officially starting at the school, I met individually with key members of staff to get under the skin of the situation. This enabled me to make an immediate impact when I joined. Staff were slightly surprised when I asked them to provide me with advice. However, everyone had an opinion of what the school should be doing better. The experience was informative yet reassuring. I would certainly recommend it to anyone undertaking a change of role or first headship.

It became apparent that the staff had a genuine desire and hunger to turn things around. Overwhelmingly, they were concerned about the lack of substantive leadership, which for over twelve months had left the school in a period of limbo. Nearly all members of the leadership team were in temporary roles, and as a result it must have been very challenging for them to genuinely exert their influence over the future direction of the school. It became clear that addressing this area would be a significant priority. However, it was an investment of time which ensured staff could express their views and see that I would be open and approachable.

Within my first week at the school in June 2019, we opened a formal consultation on a permanent leadership team structure. By the end of the summer term, with the support of a strong governing body and an excellent chair of governors who was prepared to take bold decisions, we had appointed a new leadership team. This included a head of school who joined from another school. I am certain that staff were surprised at the pace of action. However, it reinforced our ambitions, and since many staff had recommended this as part of their pre-discussions, it demonstrated that we would listen and, more importantly, act.

The second phase, which began in the autumn term, sought to address medium-term challenges. Having really good heads of school in both schools enabled me to shift my leadership style. As a leadership team, we were able to take on a more collaborative approach, whilst making sure that staff at all levels were able to help move the school in the right direction. Throughout this period, clear and consistent communication was going to be needed to secure the necessary buy-in from staff.

A key area of our improvement work was linked to the quality of teaching. There were pockets of excellent and very good practice at the school, but it was inconsistent within and across departments. We explained that the removal of high-stakes activities, such as issuing judgements for lesson observations and conducting department reviews, were to reduce unnecessary anxiety amongst staff. Constantly modelling the expectations we wished to see from teachers and other staff was effective in building trust. We explained that we would move to a more formative model, where leaders would coach staff and they could work collaboratively with peers to enable everyone to improve their practice. I describe it as 'catching staff doing things well' and explicitly celebrating success, rather than looking for mistakes.

By the time the partnership had entered the third phase of development, we had already seen huge improvements. By January 2020, the use of early entry meant the proportion of Year 11 students who had already secured a good grade in English and mathematics had risen by 10% from 2018. At the same time, our progress data was already well above expectations. Then we were hit by the global health crisis. On reflection, this was a leveller for the partnership as a whole – a blank page and a genuine opportunity for collaboration. Up until this point, the partnership had been largely centred on a model of shared executive leadership, and whilst there had been some collaboration between staff at the two schools, it was more piecemeal. However, to navigate through the sheer volume of work as a result of the pandemic, I felt we needed to change the relationship to a model where we were genuinely learning together. Eighteen months earlier, we would have been duplicating activities in each school, and had COVID not happened we may not have progressed to this model at the same speed. There has been a genuine desire to build programmes together and, in many ways, this has seen growth in the staff of both schools.

The greatest challenge I have found throughout this change process, as a leader, has been my ability to let go. I am the sort of person who loves detail and being involved in the working of the school. Recognising and accepting that my role has evolved is tough. I am still uncertain as to whether I am comfortable with this, and I have to remind myself that my role is now about ensuring that the leaders and staff in both schools are living out the expectations and values to which we subscribe. I cling to the hope that the nature of the role may evolve further once the immediate pressures of the pandemic pass. I guess, for me, this will potentially be the fourth phase.

How do we stay tuned into our context, even after a number of years in the same organisation?

Reading the external and internal context and observing subtle but important changes that may require a new approach is highly important. What makes it even more challenging is that it may involve us having to question the appropriateness of systems and processes that we have personally introduced and which have worked very well for quite a few years, or it may require us to question the behaviours of colleagues we have personally appointed and who have served the organisation well in the past.

There are lots of good things about being an experienced leader compared to a novice. Experienced leaders can draw on their previous experience and knowledge; they have mental maps on what they know to do in this situation or that situation. All of this is good, and it is how we acquire wisdom in leadership, but we can get a bit stuck sometimes. We can become narrow in our thinking, especially if we have been in the same school or organisation for a long time. Like teachers, leaders can form habits that become instinctive. This can make it harder for leaders to change in the future.

One of the best approaches to assessing your context is to practise unbiased processing. By that, we mean objectively examining the evaluative information you have about your organisation, without exaggerating or minimising the implications (Lakey et al., 2008). It is less difficult in a new context – for example, when you move jobs – because you have fresh eyes. It is easier to ask curious and open-ended questions. It is easier to be objective about the quality of education being provided in the school. But over time, it is also easy to become overly accustomed to what you see and accept in your context, sometimes failing to notice when things change. To practise unbiased processing, you have to accept both positive and negative information about the context in which you are leading, without minimising the negative information or inflating the positive, or indeed ignoring the positive and overstating the negative.

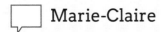 Marie-Claire

When I first became the executive head teacher of Benjamin Adlard Primary School in Gainsborough, which had recently been judged to be inadequate by the inspectorate in England (Ofsted), I knew that I was going to be leading in a new context. If I am honest, I was very nervous about whether I had enough experience as a leader to guide this school forwards towards a good inspection judgement. I was particularly worried that the staff at Benjamin Adlard would expect me to arrive with solutions, plans and ideas – none of which I had, yet!

On arrival at the school, I set up a series of one-to-one meetings with the staff team, and I asked them what they thought I needed to focus on to help the school improve. I wanted to hear their perspective of their context and what their expectations of me were.

One particular conversation really helped me to understand the environment in which I was leading. A senior member of staff very politely and respectfully said, 'Whatever you think you know about how to make schools good, it won't work here. Whatever worked in other places, it won't work here.' He meant it as a kind warning – essentially stating, 'Don't assume that you know what will work.' I really valued his candour and from that point I adjusted my approach. I would work with the team to develop solutions together, rather than feel I needed to provide all of the answers and solutions myself.

Imperfect leaders find ways to listen to what the context requires, and they do this regularly through conversation and reflection. They allow their assumptions to be challenged, which enables them to make better decisions; to adapt and change in response. Really effective leaders can 'move between contexts, address frequent changes in their context and adapt their behaviours and actions to these changes' (Shamir, 2013, p. 348).

To make things even more challenging for leaders, it is not just the context of the situation that changes; it is also, very often, the people too. As members of our senior team come and go, we may need to adapt our leadership approach in order to get the best out of them. Our role as leaders is to help our team to be the best they can be. This means that we should not be too quick to judge if a new senior colleague does certain things better or worse than their predecessor. We understand that everyone is imperfect, including our senior colleagues, and that as new people come into the team, we need to adapt our own approach to best meet the needs of those we lead.

A previous team member may not have needed much support or advice, but a new team member may need the complete opposite. A previous team member may have needed to be constantly challenged and pushed, whereas a new team member may need to be slowed down – or vice versa. Leaders who think they are perfect, or who think they have to appear to be perfect, may be tempted to believe that the context is irrelevant, that everyone should adapt themselves to their leadership. In contrast, imperfect leaders ask themselves, 'How is my context changing and what does that new context require of me as a leader?' and 'What does this member of my team now require from me as a leader if they are to be the best they can be?'

In the following case study, Alex Smith tells how he adapted his leadership to a new context. By focusing on listening to the different needs of his colleagues and recognising their strengths, it helped him to develop the strategy that would lead to significant improvement in a school that was at 'rock bottom'.

 ## Case study

Alex Smith, head teacher, Gaer Primary and Maesglas Primary, Newport, Wales

In February 2019, I was invited by the local authority to act as caretaker head teacher in Maesglas Primary, another local primary school within our cluster of schools. This would mean that I would act as executive head teacher across two schools for a fixed-term period of six weeks in the first instance. The school has 270 pupils on roll, of whom 40% on average qualify for free school meals, and it was the only 'red category' school in the city. (In the Welsh Government's accountability system for rating schools, red is the lowest category.) The head teacher had left the school at short notice. I agreed to undertake the role in a caretaking capacity initially. Following a period of success, the executive head teacher role was then advertised on a fixed-term two-year basis. I applied and was appointed. The fixed-term has now been extended and I am continuing in my role as executive head teacher.

Playing to my strengths –
demonstrating unfailing optimism

It was apparent from the outset that morale at the school was at rock bottom. There was a feeling amongst staff that the school had been unfairly judged and had been pulled in numerous directions, always being 'done to'. In their opinion, whatever they did was judged to be wrong and ineffective. It was so important to both acknowledge and empathise with these feelings as part of understanding the context.

I was aware that my initial interface with the staff would be crucial and that the first few months would be the key to earning their trust and respect. I was mindful during those first days and months that my primary goal would be to raise team morale and to shape a new and positive outlook. I was also keen to ensure that the past was not dismissed and that we identified the positive things that had been happening across the school. I have always been conscious that when a school is judged red, there are many good and excellent things to celebrate. Similarly, when graded green (the best judgement), there are always things to improve. It was important that we didn't become obsessed with a colour rating but that we took charge of our own destiny.

I have always been aware that people are the most important part of a school. It is vital that we understand the context of the people we serve and manage change well. I spent time getting to know everybody, and during these conversations I demonstrated unfailing optimism. I knew this was a strength of mine and that the optimism was never unfounded. It was evident that there were many good things happening and that staff were hard-working, committed to the school and eager to do well. There was so much to build on.

In the first few months, we undertook a range of self-evaluation exercises with the aim of recognising strengths across the school and publicly celebrating them. Writing and Assessment for Learning were a particular focus. Collective strengths were identified and targeted whole-school next steps were identified and acted upon. The morale shift was immediate and very powerful. This became a significant motivating factor.

Defaulting to others where I knew myself well enough to know that someone else would make a better job of it

It was crucial to build leadership capacity and the team around me. I was aware that this would become the driving force for the school. Other staff were more skilled in particular areas of the curriculum and were more knowledgeable than me in their fields. I recognised this and told them.

Existing senior leaders were given greater clarity regarding systems and platforms to lead. Middle leaders were given new and exciting opportunities. It was important to role model and pace-set, but equally necessary was the need for autonomy and empowerment. I invested time, energy and belief in the staff. Importantly, I showed trust in them.

A particular example of this was recognising the wealth of experience and expertise of our maths and numeracy leader. Although my own subject-specific background is in maths and numeracy, her expertise across the primary phase is far superior to mine. We capitalised on this knowledge. We initiated a strategic approach to delivering whole-staff training and we undertook a range of self-evaluation activities to capture strengths and next steps. The maths and numeracy leader led comprehensive professional learning sessions focused on maths mastery, mental and written strategies and reasoning. The impact of the training was significant.

We were now taking charge of our own destiny and leading from within. Staff felt empowered and we were all pulling in the same direction. The change was strategically managed and involved all staff. The distributed model of leadership created the platform for leaders to engage in collaboration, lead training, undertake self-evaluation to measure impact and celebrate successes.

Things for leaders to consider

Arguably, the single most important factor that leaders should consider when applying their leadership in a new context is that establishing and maintaining effective relationships with all stakeholders is key to success. Getting to know the people and striking the right balance between power and love will create a thriving learning environment for the whole community.

In the most challenging circumstances, it is vital to show unfailing optimism. Think carefully about where you channel your energy when strategically managing change. Think of ways to create positive energy around you so that people enjoy their work and feel valued. Be true to yourself and act with integrity, making your principles very visible. Earn the trust of your team. Never just assume it. Everyone can relate to the value of hard work. This is essential to success when faced with any new context. Listen intently to the people around you. Recognise where others are more skilled and will complement your skill set. Celebrate these strengths and allow them to lead.

Prompts for personal reflection

▦ What kind of leadership is needed from you now (compared to last year or when you first took up your current role)?

▦ What more might you do to make sure that you are noticing any changes to your external and internal context and adapting accordingly?

Summary

① Self-Awareness

and Tuning into Context

Self-awareness is at the heart of good leadership. It enables us to manage ourselves more effectively and to minimise some of the negative aspects of our own default behaviours. It is a lifelong process, but there are things we can do to further develop our own self-awareness. Those with an imperfect leadership mindset seek to adapt to their shifting context and ask themselves: 'What kind of leadership is needed from me now?'

▦ Creating a powerful culture of feedback, and asking for specific feedback as a leader, helps us to understand how others see us and deepens our self-awareness.

▦ Developing self-awareness is not just about understanding ourselves in a work context. Seeking feedback from friends and family can also help us to reflect and become aware of things that matter to us and how we manage our time and commitments.

▦ Imperfect leaders don't ignore the context in which they lead. They tune into the context and adapt their leadership appropriately.

Exercises to try

- List five aspects of your leadership that you consider to be strengths. Score each of them out of 10 as to how strong you are at them (10 being high). Now estimate how you think others would score you. Reflect on any differences (remembering the Johari window mentioned earlier in this chapter).

- Describe yourself from the following list of adjectives (pick your top six). Then ask your colleagues and friends to choose which words they think best describe you. (You can photocopy the list below and ask them to highlight the words they choose.) Reflect on any differences.

> able   accepting   adaptable   bold   brave
>
> calm   caring   cheerful   clever   complex
>
> confident   dependable   dignified   energetic   extroverted
>
> friendly   giving   happy   helpful   idealistic
>
> independent   ingenious   intelligent   introverted   kind
>
> knowledgeable   logical   loving   mature   modest
>
> nervous   observant   organised   patient   powerful
>
> proud   quiet   reflective   relaxed   spiritual
>
> responsive   searching   self-assertive   self-conscious   sensible
>
> sentimental   shy   silly   spontaneous   sympathetic
>
> tense   trustworthy   warm   wise   witty

- Share these differences with a trusted colleague and ask them, 'What strikes you about this'? Decide which areas of difference, if attended to and developed, would have the greatest impact on you and your leadership.

Chapter 2

Developing and Empowering Teams

I regard myself as a bungalow and I try to appoint skyscrapers.

Principal of a school in Switzerland

Imperfect leaders know their weaknesses as well as their strengths, so they try to appoint people who are noticeably better at things than they are. They try to ensure that the team has the balance of skills and expertise that no single person can possibly have.

Imperfect leaders see their role in developing and empowering teams as fundamental to the work, and not as an optional extra. They know that if the school is to have sustainable success, then a team that works effectively together and maximises the expertise of each person is essential. They reject the 'hero leader' model. They understand deeply that what counts is not who has the best idea at the beginning of the process but whether the right decisions are made and whether good outcomes are achieved.

Leading a team is one of the most challenging parts of our role as leaders – it is highly complex and it can be frustrating, but it can also be a delight to see a team develop and work well. However, leadership teams in schools can often lack collective effectiveness, and in some cases they can even lose the effectiveness that they once had. Here are some reasons why leadership teams can go wrong.

1. The team leader or head teacher is over-controlling

The leader allocates tasks rather than delegating responsibility and accountability. Team members are neither empowered nor supported or developed as leaders within their key areas of work.

We have come across head teachers who are so convinced that they know the right thing to do in most circumstances that they end up disempowering their teams. The team members soon realise that rather than give their views on a matter raised in the meeting, the best thing to do is to keep quiet. If they wait long enough the leader will tell them the right answer and the decision.

In more nuanced situations, we have seen leaders who are genuinely trying to delegate responsibility to their team but are so fixed on being in control (it is how they have been successful in the past) that they cannot let go. Rather than delegating responsibility, they end up delegating tasks, regularly checking the work of their colleagues and making all the most important decisions. The team members end up with the worst of both worlds: even more work but not trusted to take decisions or to think for themselves.

Of course, there are times when urgent and more hierarchical decision-making is needed. Sometimes as a leader you inherit a weak or dysfunctional team and, in that context, immediately delegating responsibility is not always the right thing to do. In times of crisis, there may be insufficient time to delegate appropriately. For example, during the pandemic many school leaders have found themselves operating in a more top-down manner than they would normally. But those with an imperfect leadership mindset know that the school will be better if there is a strong, effective and empowered team taking collective responsibility for the success of the organisation and that is what they work towards. Fundamentally, our job as leaders is to help our team – individually and collectively – to be the best they can be.

It is hard to build a system where others can succeed if the leader believes he or she needs to make every important decision and knows better than anyone else what to do and how to do it. At times, we can disempower our colleagues simply by being perceived to be too much of an expert in the issue ourselves.

Steve

Many years ago, I was leading a local education authority. Every three years, each authority in the country had to submit a high-stakes education improvement plan to the government. The plans were assessed, and if they were judged to be of high quality then resources were allocated to implement the plan. If the plans were judged to be poor or inadequate then resources were more limited and, instead, the local education authority received more focused monitoring from the government.

I had been the main author of the plan in my previous local authority and it had been judged to be very good. By the time it was due to submit the next plan, I had moved local authorities and was now the chief officer for education. I delegated this task to the appropriate senior leader in my team and gave the person a copy of my previous plan, which had received plaudits. To cut a long story short, it didn't end well.

I did some serious reflection afterwards about why it had gone wrong, and how, if I had behaved differently, there might have been a better outcome. I realised that I had come across as too much of an expert, too potentially intimidating. I had not understood sufficiently that the task I had delegated was beyond her capacity without additional help, and that she didn't have enough confidence to admit it. Instead of providing appropriate support, I had not modelled that asking for help is a strength in leadership rather than something to be embarrassed about.

The learning for me as a leader was that if we want those whom we lead to feel okay about asking for help and if we want to build trust in the organisation, then we need to model asking for help ourselves. We need to be open about the times when we ourselves lack capacity or expertise.

> **"** We asked a thousand leaders to list marble-earning behaviours – what do your team members do that earns your trust? The most common answer: asking for help. When it comes to people who do not habitually ask for help, the leaders we polled explained that they would not delegate important work to them because the leaders did not trust that they would raise their hands and ask for help. Mind. Blown. (Brown, 2018, p. 228)

2. The team is not sufficiently clear about the mission, values and overall strategy

As a result of ambiguity, priorities may conflict rather than align. If we want to build alignment and coherence in our team, it can be helpful to start with working on a mission. If we are all clear about the 'why' and about what we are committed to achieving together, this can serve as a touchpoint to refocus on when things get messy.

In a busy school where there is barely enough time to do anything properly and the urgent is coming at you at full speed, spending time on mission, on overall strategy and on values can be seen as an unnecessary luxury, but it can prove to be a great way of 'keeping the main thing the main thing'. Inevitably, a wide range of initiatives, requests and demands will come to you and your senior team, many of which may sound interesting, even compelling, and may be dear to the heart of one member of the team, but it may not be possible or desirable to prioritise them. Being clear about mission and strategy can help to keep you focused and aligned.

We know of a primary head teacher in England who spent all morning on an in-service professional development session with all the staff in the school focusing on just four questions: Who are we? Why are we here? What are we trying to achieve together? Are we all up for this? She said it was the best staff development session that had ever taken place! Of course, once this had been discussed and agreed, her next question was, 'How can we make sure we stay on track?'

Note

When Lina Al Naccache became the head teacher at Ras Beirut Secondary Public School in Beirut, Lebanon, she knew that the first step to developing her team and her teachers was to get clear on the mission and vision for the school. She did this by pulling together teachers and coordinators from every department in the school to agree what their priorities needed to be and establish the vision. She didn't do this in isolation; she did it with her team. She knew that they needed her leadership, but she knew her leadership was not sufficient on its own.

3. Not having the right people in the room

People are often present because of their role rather than their expertise on the issues being addressed. At any given time, the person in the organisation with the most expertise on the issue being discussed may not even be in the room. This can be a real weakness with executive teams.

 Steve

Not having the right people in the room is something I got wrong quite a few times in my leadership. I wasn't always good enough at forward planning to make sure that I had considered who needed to be there (in addition to members of the senior leadership team) for strategic discussions on particular items. We always need to ask ourselves for any given meeting: 'Who else needs to be here for this?'

4. It is the head teacher's meeting, not mine

People can think it is the head teacher's meeting and his or her responsibility to make it work, not theirs. Therefore, they tend to do scant preparation and give the agenda little prior thought. This may well be the default mode for senior team meetings. If we want to change this, then we need to work very hard and proactively. The key is very strong delegation to others – to each member of the team, not just to some – so that, increasingly, there is collective accountability. It requires constant vigilance, which is hard when everyone is so busy.

5. Poor behaviour

Poor behaviour includes turning up late, sending apologies at the last minute, being disrespectful about children/young people/their parents, being rude to/about a colleague, using 'humour' that makes others feel uncomfortable and so on. If this is not challenged and confronted, it will continue. This can be addressed by agreeing on some basic processes or ground rules for how the team will work together and by making sure that you have a word with anyone who doesn't keep to them (as soon as possible – don't put it off, even if it seems to be a minor issue).

6. Lack of clear outcomes and actions

At the end of the meeting there can be a lack of well-defined, strategic decisions, with no specific actions or allocation of responsibility. Summing up at the end of the meeting, agreeing actions and deadlines, and recording and following up on those actions to ensure that deadlines are met is crucial. Without this, meetings can become talking shops – not only a waste of time but also frustrating and counterproductive. Finding a way to build agreed outcomes, next steps and deadlines into the meeting itself can save so much time and stress later.

7. Groupthink

After a while, many teams can get so used to working together that they develop a kind of groupthink – they all start to see things in the same way. There is hardly any disagreement and decisions are always unanimous. This can be a worrying situation for a leader. It can lead to complacency and to decisions that are not thought-through carefully enough. In these situations, it is important to encourage challenge by considering and discussing what others who might disagree with the decision would argue and how they would feel. It is also good to welcome challenge into the team through inviting other leaders or external consultants to some meetings, in order to provide some external perspectives.

8. Focusing on the urgent

In busy, fast-moving and time-poor organisations, the urgent and operational can too easily dominate the important and strategic. Operational issues usually require less preparation and less thinking in advance, so they are easier to discuss than strategic issues. What is more, the urgent can be attractive: you can feel positive about agreeing the actions and ticking off the fact that they have been completed. This has often been the case during the pandemic, as leaders have had to focus on managing things that are not easy to control and require an immediate response. But even at a time of crisis and uncertainty, it is critical that we build in some time for strategic planning. We tend to put the important off because the urgent has to be dealt with and, as a result, we too often find that we don't get to the issues that matter the most. If possible, try to agree that at every meeting there will be at least one big strategic and long-term issue on the agenda (and that the right people are in the room to discuss it).

9. Trust between team members can be lacking

An absence of reciprocity and generosity within and outside meetings can lead to tensions. If there is trust you can cut corners and get things done fast and powerfully. If there is limited trust it can be stressful and painful.

In the following case study, Maureen Nugent describes how she changed her leadership approach in order to develop and empower the teams she leads – including empowering students and their families. She describes a seminal moment when she began to shift her leadership attitude and, in her words, 'let go' – trusting and allowing others the opportunity to lead and making sure she had the right people in the room. What we love about the story she tells is how grounded it is in her values as a leader. Imperfect leaders, like Maureen, develop teams who are empowered and trusted, as well as accountable and responsible.

 # Case study

Maureen Nugent, head teacher, St Brendan's Primary School, Glasgow, Scotland

For the past eight years, I have been a head teacher in Glasgow working in St Brendan's Primary School. As part of the Excellence in Headship programme, run by Education Scotland, I attended a values-based leadership event led by Columba 1400. This changed my thinking both in personal and professional terms. Norman Drummond shared his words of wisdom: 'Continue to keep shining, and in doing so subconsciously you will give others the permission to do the same.' This was the pivotal moment when I consciously began to think differently. This message has been by far the single most important thread in the transformation of pupils and of staff leadership at St Brendan's Primary School.

Our preferred future vision was clear: 'Let's shine brightly together … moving forward and improving together.' Our school priority, based on our most recent school inspection, was to raise attainment, recognise achievement and support well-being. The big question for pupils, staff and families to consider was: how can we move from good to great? If we were going to achieve this, we knew that it was essential that each of the constituents that make up our family team – pupils, colleagues and families – had a chance to contribute and to shine. Through our commitment to self-evaluation, we began to elicit views from all of our family team.

- **Pupils.** Pupils' rights are promoted throughout the school. They are displayed in all classrooms and we have a children's rights committee who lead this area across the school. Pupils' voices are encouraged and promoted across all aspects of school life. They regularly participate in class self-evaluation on school improvement – for example, our P7 pupils (10–11-year-olds) made a request to sit on chairs instead of wooden benches during school assemblies. This request was relatively easy to solve compared to the request for the school to have a swimming pool! We were the first ever school in Scotland to co-design a Values-Based Leadership Academy for our P7 pupils. The children actively seek out leadership opportunities across the school to lead the learning – for example, they delivered lessons to the whole school and increased awareness around the well-being indicators.

- **Colleagues.** In addition to our informal/formal interactions with staff, there are weekly staff meetings – our favourite part of the week is our informal get-together before work: tea, toast and tasteful conversation. Through our annual professional review and development coaching process, we create opportunities for conversation and dialogue around individual strengths, interests and areas for personal/professional growth. By taking time to show an interest in individuals, and by demonstrating trust, we have been able to encourage and nudge colleagues in the right direction so that they will use their own talents and have the courage to step out and lead. Our collegiate evaluation groups engage in reflection and continuous self-evaluation. How do we move from good to great? What will we start, stop and continue? Our career-long professional learning provides opportunities for a wide range of courses that staff can attend.

- **Families.** St Brendan's families are supportive and engage in the life of the school. In addition to the school's parent council, we have set up a family improvement team who have worked in collaboration with school staff to lead on areas from the school improvement plan. They organised a series of visits to the school by other interested parents to share their skills and experiences to support the development of the young workforce. There are regular opportunities for families to share their views on all aspects of school life. We have a motto: 'We ask, you say and we do.' We also plan a yearly overview of fun activities to engage with parents.

Our whole-school approach to leadership is now more visible. Our young people, in particular our P7 pupils, demonstrate an increase in knowledge, skills and confidence as they lead initiatives across the school. All staff, regardless of their remit or job title, are encouraged to take on leadership opportunities, thus opening pathways for many staff who have gone on to further develop their own leadership journey. Families have shown a willingness to share their own skills and experience with our children and staff.

I have learned to be true to myself, and to others, and to have the confidence to think about and act on the things that I really care about in life. I understand and accept that I am an imperfect leader, recognising my own strengths and weaknesses. By developing a culture of trust, I can let go and, by doing so, allow others to have opportunities to shine. And I can take pleasure in their successes, thus building a stronger family team. As a leader of learning, my journey is far from over.

My advice to other school leaders is to promote and develop the 'one big family' culture and an inclusive school climate where everyone matters. Then the shared vision comes alive. Involve everyone in self-evaluation, ask challenging questions and allow headspace for individuals to think. Help to create what Columba 1400 describe as 'chill and still moments' and seek opportunities for colleagues to share views and work collaboratively.

As imperfect leaders, we can paint the picture of a preferred future. We can dance as a solo performer, but we can also enjoy the group routine – supporting, encouraging and motivating others to do well.

Building trusting teams

There is a growing body of research which indicates that the level of trust in an organisation is directly related to the organisation's capacity to improve. In their seminal study on the reform efforts of twelve Chicago public schools, Anthony Bryk and Barbara Schneider (2003) found that enabling positive social relationships between adults was the key to successful school improvement – and that trust was at the heart of those relationships. As leaders, we all want to be trusted, but at times it is easy to forget that trust must be earned and actively developed; it cannot be assumed or neglected. We believe that imperfect leaders are trust creators in their organisations, building trustworthy teams.

There are four basic elements of trust. Firstly, the people we lead must be able to trust in our *capability* and *competence* as leaders. If we want to be trusted, then we must be committed to doing our job well and learning how to be even more effective in the future. Secondly, our colleagues must be able to trust that we are reliable and that we keep our promises. This is sometimes called *contractual trust*. Just like the motto of the London Stock Exchange, imperfect leaders are able to say, 'My word is my bond.' The third element of trust is built through our *communication*. Trust is built when leaders are able to be honest, show openness, and act and speak with authenticity. Finally, the fourth element of trust could be described as *committed trust*. This form of trust is evident in leaders who show goodwill and kindness towards those they lead, in leaders who are consistent in making decisions based on what is best for the organisation and for the people they lead, and in leaders who are committed to the vision of the organisation.

In developing and empowering teams, leaders must first model trustworthiness and cultivate trustworthiness in their team.

 ## Marie-Claire

It is possible to assess the levels of trust in schools. A real opportunity for growth came for me as a leader, and my senior leadership team, when we undertook an audit of trust in our school, based on examples of trust audits shared by David Hargreaves (2012). We conducted a survey and asked our whole staff to what extent they agreed or disagreed with a series of about 100 statements that indicate levels of trust – for example:

- Leaders always keep their promises.

- Colleagues show goodwill towards me.

- My colleagues always keep their promises.

- I am able to be honest.

- Leaders are honest with me.

- I am listened to.

- I trust the members of my team.

- My colleagues always do what they say they will do.

- I always keep my promises.

- Leaders are consistent.

This opened up valuable conversations within our senior team about how we build trust through everyday interactions and conversations with staff at all levels. Are we consistent as leaders? Do we always do what we say we will do and follow up on things?

We have both had experiences of trying to build trust in a leadership team when some members of the team trusted each other wholeheartedly and others did not.

Some members of your team might be on exactly the same wavelength with you. You have complete trust in them, as they do with you. As a result, you can cut corners and move things forward at pace. With others in the team there may be a reasonable amount of trust and certainly no major barriers, but there is occasionally some wariness. In some cases there could be a significant lack of trust, and perhaps even some real tensions.

Try to map out where the individual members of your team might be in terms of trust. Ask yourself: what kind of changes in my own behaviour and leadership might help to create more trust? Put yourself in their shoes. Why might they be feeling like this? Our experience is that in this kind of situation, where there are varying levels of trust in the team, it is important for the leader of the team to model the kinds of behaviour that build trust:

- Admitting mistakes.

- Asking for help and seeking advice.

- Valuing the expertise of others.

- Welcoming feedback and challenge.

Why is trust so important for developing and empowering teams?

The term 'social capital' was first used by Lyda Hanifan over 100 years ago when he wrote about how communities work best together. He described it as 'those tangible assets [that] count for most in the daily lives of people: namely goodwill, fellowship, sympathy, and social intercourse among the individuals and families who make up a social unit' (Hanifan, 1916, p. 130). Professor David Hargreaves (2001) outlines how social capital and high levels of trust create strong professional relationships in a school, and how this in turn creates intellectual capital – that is, employee expertise, knowledge and skills.

We believe that in order to develop and empower teams, it is critical to develop trust between members of the team. In order to build a sustainable team, we believe that you should begin by creating a culture where leaders freely show goodwill to one another. Some leaders have made the mistake of creating a culture within which the team are overly dependent on the leader for approval.

Sometimes, team members may even feel they need to compete for the leader's attention. This isn't healthy; to create a sustainable and empowered team we need to be able to connect team members with one another in positive ways. Once goodwill is formed between members of your team, the team will be able to be more open and honest with one another and, in turn, this develops the reliability as well as the competence that commands respect. Trust is built slowly, especially for leaders who may have to share fears and anxieties, as well as their hopes and aspirations, about their leadership practice.

Trust leads to reciprocity – that is, the sense of sharing and obligation towards mutual exchange. For example, if I offer you a gift or help, you feel you want to make some kind of return to me. Reciprocity arises when there is a certain degree of trust, perhaps no more than just goodwill; but once it takes place, the level of trust increases. Trust and reciprocity are mutually dependent and, in practice, reinforce each other in a virtuous circle. One feeds the other. As leaders, it is important that we model this.

> **"** If leaders believe that followers first have to earn trust, they actually will foster mistrust. You have to invest in trust *before* people have earned it. Trust is a verb before it becomes a state. (Fullan, 2018, pp. 84–85)

When social capital (i.e. trust and reciprocity) between colleagues in your team is at a high level, they will begin to share and grow their intellectual capital – that is, their knowledge and skills. Figure 2.1 below represents this process, and the key characteristics of both trust and reciprocity, which produces intellectual capital.

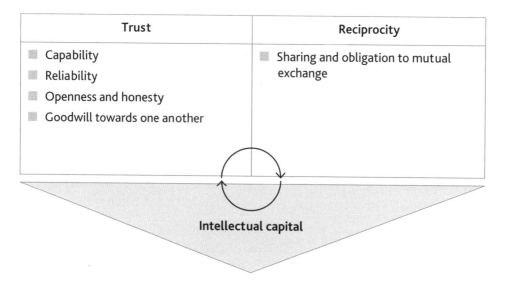

Trust	Reciprocity
▦ Capability ▦ Reliability ▦ Openness and honesty ▦ Goodwill towards one another	▦ Sharing and obligation to mutual exchange

Intellectual capital

Figure 2.1. Trust + reciprocity = high social capital

When all members of a team believe they have something to offer to others and something to gain from others, social capital is built further. We can model this as imperfect leaders, highlighting how others contribute to our own learning and development.

In addition to trust, Amy Edmondson argues that we also need to develop psychologically safe work environments. She says: 'trust is about giving people the benefit of the doubt, and psychological safety relates to whether others will give you the benefit of doubt when, for instance, you have asked for help or admitted a mistake' (Edmondson, 2019, p. 17). The question this raises is the extent to which leaders are able to be genuinely open about sharing areas of failure, weakness or poor performance, as well as whether they are able to stretch beyond their organisational boundaries to ask for or offer help.

Imperfect leaders know that they don't know it all, but that by creating trustworthy relationships between colleagues they can mobilise intellectual capital to achieve the desired educational outcomes, and they can ask for help when they need it.

Marie-Claire

In their book, *The Speed of Trust*, Stephen Covey and Rebecca Merrill describe thirteen behaviours of high trust. I found these extremely helpful for opening up conversations about how to develop trust in teams. In short, Covey and Merrill (2006, p. 143) say that to build trust in our teams we need to: 'Be honest. Tell the truth. Let people know where you stand. Use simple language. Call things what they are. Demonstrate integrity. Don't manipulate people or distort facts. Don't spin the truth. Don't leave false impressions.'

I used the thirteen behaviours with one particular team I was leading to help us develop trust. Firstly, we reviewed together how well we were doing as a team in relation to the behaviours. I then asked team members to say which behaviour they wanted to see more of in the team and which behaviour they were going to focus on themselves. Over time, we got much better at talking straight to one another in the room rather than behind closed doors and outside of meetings. We also improved on how well we learned together as a team and regularly took time out to reflect and develop our skills as leaders.

Prompts for personal reflection

What has resonated with you in the last section on building trust in teams? How could you turn this into a prompt for personal reflection? For example:

▪ In what ways do you actively build trust and encourage goodwill between colleagues?

▪ Do leaders in your school (including you) always keep commitments and do what you say you will do?

▪ How do your colleagues know that you trust them? What do you do which shows that?

▪ Are you open to listening to and understanding the views and perspectives of others?

▪ Do you delegate both responsibility and accountability, or do you just delegate tasks?

▪ Have you created a culture where people can talk straight and say what they think?

Imperfect leaders develop and empower their team without losing sight of the impact on the front line

In *The Five Dysfunctions of a Team: A Leadership Fable*, Patrick Lencioni (2002) tells the story of a new CEO at a technology company. Her task is to build the senior executive leadership into an effective and high-functioning team. The book describes five dysfunctions that lead to team ineffectiveness: absence of trust, fear of conflict, lack of commitment, avoidance of accountability and inattention to results. The model that Lencioni presents at the end is a practical framework for leaders who want to create an effective team. One of the focus points for the new CEO in Lencioni's fable is the concept of defining the 'first team'. The CEO reminds her senior executive that as team members they have a collective common purpose which supersedes their individual department priorities. She asks the team to put team results ahead of everything else. She is clear with them that the senior executive team should be their first team.

However, we would argue that as an imperfect leader you must simultaneously develop your first team without losing sight or connection with the front line. At times, leadership teams can become too insular and there can be a danger of groupthink (see reason number 7 of why teams go wrong, on page 34), when leaders are cut off from candid communication from the wider organisation. People outside the team may perceive members of the team to be inaccessible or unapproachable. It is also possible that the team may become so focused on themselves and their effectiveness that they do not consider adequately how decisions are cascaded and translated. As a result, implementation can be poor. This is particularly challenging in bigger organisations where leaders can become overly reliant on the team as their eyes and ears on the ground.

We believe that as leaders we have to get the balance right between trusting the team to get on with the job and developing a culture of quality assurance, where triangulation and collective responsibility for quality and impact is everyone's responsibility. Imperfect leaders need to remain obsessed with the front-line experience of learning for our children and young people, using every opportunity to interact with teachers and students, to learn with them, and to avoid silo thinking and groupthink.

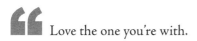 Love the one you're with.

Stephen Stills

We need to consider one final aspect of building and empowering teams in this chapter. Leaders can sometimes inherit a weak or even dysfunctional team. As the new head teacher, perhaps we think that the team may have been right for the previous context but isn't necessarily right for the challenges ahead under our leadership. When we go into a new school, we may find that we don't like some members of our team. This can make us hanker after a different team – perhaps more like the one we left behind in our previous job, where trust had been built and effective ways of working were well established. The good news is that we don't have to like each member of our team; we just have to form a professional, trusting relationship with them. It might be a very good thing for the school that a particular member of the team has a different way of looking at things than we do.

Of course, it is right for leaders to want the best and, over time, to replace team members with individuals who have the expertise and approach that is needed for the future. Similarly, a fundamental clash of values may be impossible to resolve. However, changing the personnel in a team may take some time and we cannot afford for the school to stagnate in the meantime. We have to work on our mindset as leaders, to be wary of making early judgements about individuals and to do all that we can to develop trust.

We have found it helpful to try to empathise with our team members, to spend some time walking in their shoes and to understand their motivations and drivers. In most cases, the team members who seem to us to be problematic will have had some success in the past. Perhaps they have lost confidence or have become stuck in a rut. Sometimes, we find that if we allocate a new role to a team member that really connects with their drivers and expertise, and helps them to rebuild their confidence, those individuals we initially thought were incompetent or unhelpful can excel and we can develop strong and powerful relationships with them.

In the final case study in this chapter, Rabiathul Bazriya shares the approach she took to developing and empowering leaders in a large primary school in Singapore. In Singapore, principals are rotated by the Ministry of Education every five to seven years, and you don't always get a choice about the school to which you are moved. School leaders know that they must develop the team they have inherited, whilst being confident that when they move on to their next school, that the team will be in a good position and ready for a new leader. We think this case study is a great example of a leader who understands the importance of collective leadership – creating effective team leaders and team players through shared language, vision and strategies which ensure that no one in the team is indispensable.

 ## Case study

Rabiathul Bazriya, principal, Evergreen Primary School, Singapore

2021 marked the eleventh year of my journey as a school principal, but I have been in the teaching service for thirty years or so. The journey has been peppered with its fair share of exhilaration and satisfaction as well as exasperation and anxieties. As I reminisce about my teaching career, I appreciate the diverse positions from which I have led – starting as a classroom teacher, then head of department, vice principal and, finally, as a principal in as many as six different types of school. This has undoubtedly influenced and shaped who I am today.

In Singapore's teaching service, one does not apply for the position of school principal; instead, when we first become appointed as a teacher, we can develop on one of the three available tracks – Teaching Track, Leadership Track or Specialist Track. Based on our performance and potential, we are selected for interviews for the different school leadership appointments over our career. As principals, we are rotated every five to seven years in the public schools, so as to allow for new experiences and expertise to be shared and to add to the richness of the current culture.

When I first stepped into Seng Kang Primary School as a newly appointed school principal, the harsh reality that every decision stops with me hit me hard. From critical decisions concerning finance, curriculum and pedagogical matters, staff deployment and development, estate management, to pupil development and management, and partnerships, the principal is accountable for every decision made. I also needed to be cognisant that school leadership included the ability to lead nationally by being sensitive to national issues and policies and cascading them strategically into school curricula and programmes and nuancing it appropriately to the school population.

The mind-boggling and pertinent question was, what does the new school principal start with? Do I continue with the old practices and policies for six months or a year before I start introducing innovative changes? What if the people in the current institution become so comfortable that they become averse to changes later? Will I get their buy-in to new ideas? Or will they be reticent to the fact that a new broom sweeps clean and do whatever the leader wants them to do mindlessly? Do I seek to be understood first, or make changes and let experience and results speak for themselves? Actually, no guru is able to coach us precisely on what is the right thing to do first, as every leader's school context, strengths and personality vary.

Building the individual and the team

My personal mantra is the importance of collective leadership and that no one should be indispensable. In my current school, Evergreen Primary, instead of simply relying on my current middle managers (MMs) alone, I decided to proactively grow and develop the next two tiers of leaders within the school, so there is always a team of MMs to lead to ensure school sustainability and stability.

This desire to develop my MMs gave birth to a programme called SHINE – Supporting Officers with High Potential. Staff with potential to become MMs or specialist teachers were identified early and customised professional development modules were conducted for them over two years. Growing the confidence and self-efficacy of potential MMs before they assume positions is very important for their peers to accept them as leaders. With the success of the previous programme, SHINE 2.0 started this year with another group of eight energetic, sincere and committed teachers with the potential to be nurtured to become the next set of leaders. As they grow together, they also develop a sense of teamwork and camaraderie. This deep sense of collaboration instead of competition and a sense of common purpose and goals have become the work norm amongst them. Undoubtedly, the school has benefited from this approach.

For an organisation to grow, power and decision-making cannot reside only with the school leaders or MMs. Teachers and pupils must feel empowered to have 'choice and voice', so that they feel a sense of belonging and accountability to the institution.

As well as running our school as a whole, we also run it by levels of learning in different blocks, which include two floors of the school building. The heads of year conceptualise the theme, culture and practices for the area of the school they are responsible for in alignment with school directions. They assess pupils' needs, financial and socio-economic status, special educational needs and behavioural needs before designing programmes that are customised to meet the needs of the pupils in their particular block. As a result, teachers from the whole block get involved in the learning, development and well-being of all the pupils.

Instead of a 'my class' attitude, the school culture has evolved into 'our class, our pupils' vocabulary. The respective teachers of each level hold weekly discussions during scheduled time to update pupil well-being and discipline matters and to monitor pupil learning across the various disciplines. They organise platforms to celebrate success and share good stories, so the pupils in the block feel that they belong.

What did I learn as a leader?

School leadership is both an art and a science. Whilst there are many books that share tips and strategies on what a principal should do, it is still highly dependent on the context, strengths, competencies and persona of the leader in charge. The educational landscape of the respective countries also influence how schools should respond to the changes and needs of the nation. The current pandemic is one such strong example. As a leader, it is critical that I am nimble and adaptable to ever-changing global and national needs, so that instead of playing catch-up, the school that I am leading is on top of the curve. For that, I have to understand and be humble about my own limitations as a principal.

No two school contexts, cultures and people are the same, and thus experience can become a double-edged sword if I assume that I can cut and paste what was successful from my previous school, Seng Kang Primary, to Evergreen Primary, where I am now. As a school principal's stint typically lasts from five to seven years, my commitment will always be to develop people and teams for the next principal to build upon. The pillars keeping the school strong will be the MMs and teacher leaders.

My leadership stance has evolved over the years. Initially, I started my journey leading from the front – envisioning and formulating the school's vision, mission and values, developing the MMs and ensuring there is visibility for me as the school principal. When the policies and sound processes had been in place consistently and people were clear of the school goals, I shifted and led from the side, guiding, probing and advising when the need arose. Now, after five years in my current school, I can confidently declare that I have moved and started leading from the back because the MMs and teacher leaders are confident and competent. My role is to ensure that I shepherd them in the right direction and continue to inspire and motivate them, so that they stay aligned with the larger vision and purpose as we lead the school in deepening the school culture, deepening our beliefs and values, deepening our processes and policies, deepening our mastery and competency, and deepening our collaboration and teamwork.

Summary

Developing and
Empowering Teams

Imperfect leaders know that they need others. They know that they will make better decisions, develop better plans and be more effective when they have harnessed the expertise and insights of team members. In order to achieve this, imperfect leaders keep a close eye on how effective their teams are. They take personal responsibility for creating the right culture and environment for team members to thrive. This involves:

- Developing deep levels of trust by ensuring that we (and members of our teams) are capable, reliable and committed.

- Modelling the right behaviours – for example, asking for help, making sure the right people are involved in decision-making, delegating effectively and preparing well for meetings.

- Developing a clear mission and strategy and communicating this well, so that team members know what they are responsible and accountable for and are working towards a shared goal.

- Ensuring that the team are focused on the right things and that meetings are purposeful and impactful.

- Developing teams and leaders at all levels of the school.

Exercises to try

- Undertake a trust survey and reflect on how to actively develop trust in your teams.

- Ask people to consider together what the team is like when it is performing at its best. Then discuss what those behaviours are and how you might be able to encourage them to happen more often.

- Discuss with your team the list of reasons why teams go wrong at the beginning of this chapter, and try to find consensus on what might be done to prevent any of these happening in your team.

Chapter 3
Asking for Help

Don't be afraid to ask for help when you need it. I do that every day. Asking for help isn't a sign of weakness, it's a sign of strength.

Barack Obama

Imperfect leaders are invitational in their approach. They ask for help and are not afraid to admit that they need it.

In the early 1960s, before most serving school leaders were born, the Beatles had a large number of hit singles. Most of them had very superficial titles like 'She Loves You' and 'I Want to Hold Your Hand'. But in 1965 they had a hit with a very different song – it was called 'Help!' The lyrics describe self-confidence draining away, leading to feelings of insecurity and a lack of self-assurance. On a positive note, the person in the song eventually realises that they need help and asks for it. However, it is not unusual for school leaders to be slow at acknowledging that they need support.

There are lots of reasons why school leaders feel that they don't want to ask for help. Sometimes it is because of a fear that it might be misinterpreted as a sign of weakness, or incompetence by others, or contribute to their own feelings of weakness. In other cases, it might be a fear that it could harm their image as a leader or damage their credibility in the eyes of the team. More often, it is because as leaders we believe that we should already know what to do and what decision to make in every situation. Would asking for help expose an inadequacy? Some leaders are afraid that asking for help might feel like an imposition, and we wouldn't want to burden others with our problems or dilemmas. Of course, leaders who *never* know what to do and who ask for help on everything may develop a credibility problem. But, overall, asking for help is good for leaders and good for the organisations they lead.

Research supports the view that a culture of help-seeking in teams contributes to positive results in a number of areas, including leadership (Edmondson, 2002). In the previous chapter, we referred to the work of Amy Edmondson in the context of building trust through creating psychological safety. She makes some powerful points about the kind of environment leaders need to create in order to learn together: 'Psychological safety means no one will be punished or humiliated for errors, questions, or requests for help, in the service of reaching ambitious performance goals. To make this work, team leaders must inspire team members to embrace error and deal with failure in a productive manner' (Edmondson, 2002, p. 22). We believe that this culture should be created and modelled by the leader. An imperfect leader is unafraid to ask for help in order to secure better learning and better decision-making.

There are a number of reasons why asking for help is a good leadership behaviour to develop.

Asking for help builds a sense of collective responsibility and is more likely to change behaviours

Top-down, directive leadership has its place in leadership, but an autocratic type of leadership is unlikely to lead to a long-term culture of collective responsibility. If, in contrast, leaders set out clear ideas about what they would like to happen, and then people are proactively invited to help co-design and shape the strategy based on their own experience and expertise, this is far more likely to lead to ownership of the outcome and more likely to change the behaviours needed to achieve that outcome. By asking for help, and by asking for others' contributions, views and ideas, we can harness the expertise and capacity of our colleagues to achieve our organisational goals.

Sometimes, if we work exceptionally hard on our own to design a wonderful new document or proposal as a way of moving the school forward, it can backfire on us. We have worked painstakingly on it to get it right and we are convinced that it will help the school to progress. We then present it to our team or to the staff as a finished document, but we have left no room for others to contribute. No matter how 'perfect' we have made the document or proposal, if there is no scope for shaping or adapting the proposal, we are less likely to build a sense of collective responsibility.

One example of the importance of invitational leadership is how leaders develop a vision for their school. When a new head teacher takes up the role, he or she is expected to have a coherent vision for the future of the school. Of course, having a vision for the school is important – those we lead don't want us to turn up and say that we have no idea what to do! – but it is also important for people to connect with the vision and have some ownership of it.

 ## Steve

Just before I started my role at the National College for School Leadership, I was invited to speak, as CEO designate, at a conference for all the staff. I told them the story of how my wife and I had heard that the view in Santorini, overlooking the blue Aegean Sea and the caldera, was supposed to be one of the most beautiful in the whole world. We organised a holiday there, flew in and rushed to the clifftop to see this wonderful view. But the mist had come down and we couldn't see anything. We knew it was a fantastic view, that the sea would be a deep blue, the buildings would be white and the caldera would be magnificent, but we just couldn't see it yet, so we couldn't say precisely what it looked like. 'In the same way,' I said to the staff, 'I have a great vision for the National College. I know it is going to be fantastic. But it is still a misty vision. I want you to work with me to clear the mist away, to firm up this vision and turn it into a reality.'

Those leaders who think that they need to be perfect will work hard on developing a vision for their organisation and present it as a finished product; in contrast, imperfect leaders are more likely to have a misty vision. They are still in charge, they are still accountable, they still provide ideas and focus, but they are invitational in approach – they invite others to help shape the thinking. In the end, a vision that is developed collaboratively is more likely to be effective, as everyone has ownership of it and can use it to guide and inform the work in the school.

Asking for help leads to better decisions and the development of more effective strategies

Asking for help from others enables us to make better decisions. Recognising that we are imperfect as leaders means that we know what we are good at and what we are not good at. It means that we are quick to seek input, guidance and support from experts, particularly in those areas where we are less confident. But it can also be incredibly powerful to ask others for their perspectives and assistance, even when we think we already know what to do. As Helen Rowland states in her case study below, 'Asking for help made me feel vulnerable, yet at the same time I felt liberated.'

 ## Case study

Helen Rowland, CEO, Focus-Trust, Oldham, England

I am proud and privileged to be the CEO of Focus-Trust, a values-based trust which runs fifteen primary schools in the North West and West Yorkshire. In the English education system there are different types of schools and groups of schools. Our group of schools is funded directly by the government. Our vision is 'Great schools at the heart of our communities', and to achieve that we employ 1,000-plus colleagues to educate and nurture our 6,000-plus children.

In March 2015, when I became the CEO, I was juggling several balls. I was the chief accounting officer, the CEO and the school improvement partner. The problem was that I didn't feel as if I was being very effective in any particular area – I had a lot to manage. Around that time, I heard John Hattie speak about his research into the concept of 'collective teacher efficacy' (Donohoo et al., 2018). Collective teacher efficacy is the belief of teachers in their ability to positively affect students; where this belief is found in schools it is strongly correlated with high student achievement. I was hooked and wanted to make this a reality across our trust. Just as schools can improve through collective commitment to all students, so too can trusts, through helping each other with a shared commitment to improving outcomes in all schools.

I shared Hattie's research with colleagues and proposed that we focus our work as a trust so that we created a culture of collective efficacy. To do this, I had to admit that I needed help. In order to achieve anything that is collective, you need everyone to know what part they need to play. I needed help from leaders, teachers and other colleagues to improve outcomes across our trust. Asking for help made me feel vulnerable, yet at the same time I felt liberated.

What we didn't know at the start was what this culture would look or feel like or what impact it might have. I asked an external facilitator to work with our senior leaders and central team to discuss and agree what we meant by collective efficacy. Through this work we created our own definition: 'A shared commitment to work together on the things that matter to improve outcomes for all.'

I believe our trust is only as strong as our weakest school, and so it was important that we all accepted a sense of moral accountability and responsibility for every school's success. When schools joined our trust, we wanted the school improvement to strengthen, and for leaders – in whatever circumstances they were in – to recognise their responsibility to contribute to the success of all schools and children in Focus-Trust. It was about changing the language to 'our schools' rather than 'my school' or 'their school'. Essentially, we wanted to create a culture where working together, asking for help and giving help was the norm.

This work led to a greater sense of ownership amongst principals, and the culture has gradually changed. We now have leaders with a deep commitment to supporting other schools and colleagues: principals release their deputies and assistant heads for secondments in other schools, deputies are members of another school's governing board, and leaders recognise that at different times, and in different aspects of school improvement, they will be 'capacity givers' and 'capacity takers', as described by Sir David Carter (Staufenberg, 2017).

In 2016, I asked the Education Development Trust's Schools Partnership Programme to help support us in establishing peer review across the trust. This was a turning point for us and central to the development of collective efficacy. As leaders, we had been anxious about asking for help and sharing our vulnerabilities. However, through peer review, our skills and confidence have been transformed and we actively embrace the extra eyes, the challenge, the coaching and the ongoing support. Asking for help through peer review is now an integral feature of our school and trust improvement cycle, and a key priority in our efforts to strengthen relationships between schools that are based on trust, honesty, mutual respect and collective efficacy.

When principals and improvement champions take part in peer reviews, they genuinely want to help the host school to learn and move forward. In our virtual peer reviews in spring 2021, our enquiry was: 'To what extent have our digital technologies contributed to improving our pedagogy, curriculum and workload efficiencies?' These reviews not only celebrated the remote education we provided through lockdown and bubble closures, and how we used technology to reduce workload, but also challenged us to ask: 'To what extent has our offer been equitable for all children?' Despite our efforts to bring vulnerable children into schools and provide devices, colleagues were honest that equity of education could improve in some cases. Subsequently, in the improvement workshops, colleagues have asked for help in identifying resources and training to ensure that all our teachers provide all our children with a quality education at all times.

Early in my career, I would try to look as if I was coping with whatever challenges I faced and often worried at night. Over time, and through experience, I have learned that it is preferable to be honest about our challenges and ask colleagues for suggestions for how we move forward together rather than looking like I have all the answers and plans. As our principals lead peer reviews and contribute to writing, monitoring and evaluating our trust's strategic plan, we all share responsibility and accountability for improvement and achieving the measures of success and milestones. I try to lead by example in having a coach in whom I confide, and I coach others beyond my organisation and outside education. Very recently, with the pending external promotion of our deputy CEO and retirement of our head of human resources, I have wondered how we will manage without them. Thus, I have been honest with our leaders and asked for their help in living out our culture of collective efficacy with their practical support.

I am grateful that collective efficacy is the glue that binds Focus-Trust together. I will always be an imperfect and invitational leader who asks for help.

In the last twenty years, research has emerged on the link between asking for help and creativity in teams. For example, Taggar (2002) notes that group creativity is improved through effective communication between group members, where providing feedback and asking for help reduces errors and finds alternative solutions. Where teams have strong help-seeking norms, levels of creativity increase. As imperfect leaders, exposing our teams to the expertise and insight from others outside of our own schools can be a catalyst for new ways of thinking about our problems and creative solutions. Asking for help builds knowledge and creates new capacities for us as leaders. As imperfect leaders, we know in what areas we have expertise and when to look to others for expert advice and guidance.

However, as leaders we sometimes get put on the spot. Parents, young people and sometimes even our colleagues expect us to be able to answer their queries and respond to their concerns instantaneously. So, we do need to try to know enough to be able to manage those situations. But, we also need to be wise enough to say when we don't know the answer, and then to ask the experts when the boundaries of our knowledge and expertise are reached.

 Note

Jürgen Klopp, the manager of Liverpool Football Club, was asked questions about his view on the dangers of playing a football match just before the lockdown in England as the COVID-19 virus began to spread rapidly. He replied that, as a football manager, he was happy to answer questions about football, but it didn't make sense to him that they were asking him about COVID-19 – making the point that the journalists should ask the experts.

Steve

When I took up the role of CEO at the National College I felt very much out of my depth and I knew that I needed help. I identified four people who had significant expertise that I lacked. Fortunately, each agreed to act as a mentor to me. One had expertise in how government worked, one had expertise in large-scale strategy, one had excellent networks and one had a deep understanding of what wasn't going well in the organisation I was now leading. The combination of help that I received from these people made a very significant difference. My decision-making was better as a result of this support. It may well have been the key difference between success and failure.

In each of my leadership roles I have always had a number of mentors, depending on the context. Interestingly, I have found that the longer I am in the role, the more I need mentors, because without external mentors I can get too close to the organisation I am leading and fail to see what is actually needed. Isolated leaders – leaders who think they can do it on their own – are living dangerously; imperfect leaders seek out help and end up with better strategies as a result.

We have noticed that some people take up leadership roles without enlisting support from a mentor – someone who can provide specific advice and expert guidance. Those with an imperfect leadership mindset know that having a mentor is a key relationship where asking for help is the norm.

We have also noticed that some leaders do seem to understand the need to have a mentor, but then agree to have one allocated to them who doesn't have the expertise they need. There are also people who think there is some kind of rule that you are only supposed to have one mentor, or that you only need a mentor for the first couple of years in your new role. Imperfect leaders are astute and seek out mentors who are experts in the areas where they need help. Leadership is a difficult job to do alone. Having one or more mentors and accessing support throughout your career is essential.

Asking for help from our senior team builds trust amongst the team and encourages others to ask for help too

We have already covered this important aspect in Chapter 2.

Asking for help is important for our own physical and mental well-being

At times of crisis or challenge, many school leaders will push themselves too hard and may end up feeling extraordinarily tired and stressed. In trying to protect and support our colleagues, we often soak up the pressure ourselves and, as a result, we may eventually fall over. There is a Japanese proverb: 'Fall down seven times, get up eight.' It is important to hold on to this message. Most leaders will have times of struggle, will make mistakes and will, metaphorically, fall over. Then they rest, get up again and carry on, ready to face the next challenge.

But in some cases, it is not as simple as that. We may well need support to help us get back up again. Asking for help is crucial to our own survival. Sometimes, asking for help means that we admit to ourselves that things aren't right and we need to change things, and that is the first step to resolving the problem. In the interests of our own personal well-being, we need to be able to ask for help – from a colleague, from a friend, from a partner or family member.

 ## Prompts for personal reflection

- When was the last time you asked for help? What happened?

- What prevents you from asking for help internally or externally? What are your own barriers or fears?

- What are the signs that, for the sake of your own well-being, you need to ask for help? Can you talk to a trusted colleague or friend about how to look out for these signs and help you reach out when you need help the most?

Invitational leadership

Leaders who invite engagement are more likely to create a positive working environment for colleagues and achieve better student outcomes

If we are invitational as leaders, it can help to give colleagues a sense that they matter, that they are part of building something important beyond their individual role, that they are trusted. There are a number of reasons why people tend to become unhappy at work. Some of the most important ones to note are:

- Irrelevance: I can't see how what I am doing is relevant to the mission of the organisation. Am I making an impact?

- Anonymity: I don't feel acknowledged or understood. Do the leaders even know who I am and what I do?

- Not trusted: What I do is never good enough. I feel either told off or overly controlled.

- Not learning and developing: I'm stuck. It's boring.

David Weston at the Teacher Development Trust in England has recently published a paper which outlines five aspects of teachers' working conditions that appear most closely related to student attainment:

- Creating opportunities for effective teacher collaboration to explore student data, plan and review lessons and curricula, and plan and moderate assessments,

- Involving teachers in whole school planning, decision-making and improvement,

- Creating a culture of mutual trust, respect, enthusiasm in which communication is open and honest,

- Build a sense of shared mission, with shared goals, clear priorities and high expectations of professional behaviours and of students' learning, and

■ Facilitating classroom safety and behaviour, where … teachers feel strongly supported by senior leaders in their efforts to maintain this classroom environment. (Weston et al., 2021, p. 3)

According to this study, the culture that is likely to achieve the best student outcomes is one where teachers feel valued and involved, and where there is a sense of collaboration, collective decision-making, co-construction, shared mission and mutual respect. This, of course, correlates with the reasons why people are more likely to be happy at work. So, if we want our colleagues to enjoy their work and if we want our students to achieve the best outcomes, then being an invitational leader and enlisting their help is key.

Invitational leadership works across networks and whole systems, not just in schools

Invitational leadership is a powerful approach for those who lead networks of schools or lead from the middle of an education system. As noted by Munby and Fullan (2016), if whole systems are to improve – rather than just individual schools – then schools need to work collaboratively in networks or alliances to help lead the system. This requires school or network leaders to lead from the middle. In order to lead whole-system improvement, those who lead from the middle will need to demonstrate three different aspects of leadership:

■ *upward leadership* to influence national or state policy

■ *lateral leadership* to collaborate with other schools and ensure knowledge transfer and collective efficacy across schools

■ *institutional leadership* to ensure that staff feel valued and supported in shaping the changes in a way that is right for their school. (Munby, 2020b, p. 2)

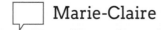 Marie-Claire

In February 2013, I became the executive head teacher of Mount Street Academy and Lincoln Carlton Academy (a new school which was due to open in September 2013). This was an internal promotion for me, as I had previously been the head of school at Mount Street. Mount Street was in a secure place: we had a stable staff team, a well-developed curriculum and standards were good. In my new role as executive head teacher, I put my energy into ensuring that the new school was ready to open in September 2013, and I assumed that Mount Street would just tick along.

In 2014, my focus shifted back to Mount Street. I had some emerging concerns that perhaps standards had slipped. As the lead school in the KYRA Teaching School Alliance, we wanted to introduce external peer review, and so I volunteered and invited a group of head teacher colleagues into the school to review how well we were doing.

One colleague head teacher, courageously and professionally, fed back that in her view we were 'heading for a disaster' with regard to phonics outcomes in Year 1. She held up a mirror and helped me and our senior team see that our context had changed in several ways and we hadn't noticed and therefore missed the chance to respond and adapt. We had three maternity leaves during 2013–2014, with newly qualified teachers covering; there was a notable change in one cohort of pupils with higher levels of special educational need and disability; and we had reduced leadership capacity as key leaders had been seconded to support the new school. We hadn't registered these changes in a way which enabled us to plan or mitigate for the impact.

The benefit of peer review was not just in helping us to become aware of an area that needed improvement; the process and outcome also empowered us to ask for help and support from the peer review team, which in turn enabled us to make rapid changes. Thankfully, phonics outcomes were much better than we had anticipated. Being able to be vulnerable and ask for help when we needed it was a powerful lever for effective collaboration in the alliance going forwards. As the lead school in the teaching school alliance, we were able to model this and open ourselves up to receive help, as well as give it. It is so useful to have someone external shine a light on your context and challenge your assumptions, but it is even more beneficial to have the support to improve by asking for help.

If a network is led by someone who regards themselves as a 'perfect leader', he or she will devise clever strategies and then direct others to implement them. This is unlikely to attract schools to want to participate. In contrast, imperfect network leaders are more likely to make themselves vulnerable and to ask for help. As Mary Hutchison demonstrates in the following case study, this behaviour attracts others to want to be part of the network and to feel they can contribute; it encourages reciprocity. Networks led by imperfect leaders may take longer to become established, but the outcome is more likely to be collective efficacy across schools rather than dependency.

 ## Case study

Mary Hutchison, principal, Roslyn Primary School, Victoria, Australia

Within eight weeks of taking up my first assistant principal position in a low socio-economic school in Victoria, Australia, the principal became very ill, ending up in intensive care. At the same time, the business manager left because her husband had a heart attack and a preparatory teacher left because her husband had been diagnosed with terminal cancer. So, after only two months at the school, I found myself in the role of acting principal.

At 9.30am on day one, a male staff member came into my office, leaned back on the chair with his arms above his head and told me that his very good friend, the sick principal, had promised him a contract next year and that I should write that down so I don't forget it. This was how he thought he could support me and the school on my first day! On my second day in charge, an aggressive father turned up at the school to beat up his daughter's teacher.

Each day, the school email system kept getting alerts about tasks not completed. I didn't even know what the tasks were or understand the implications of not doing them. I didn't know where to start. I went out to visit the 'real' principal in hospital and asked him what to do. He gave me the names of colleague principals who might help, told me what they were good at and advised me to spread the load, as they would all be very busy. I went back to school and started to ring around. I thought it would be best if I asked different people to help with different tasks, so no one would realise I really had no idea.

Every person I called came to my rescue; they couldn't wait to help. I had nothing to offer them except a thank you. Still, to this day, the principal colleagues who helped me probably do not realise how much I appreciated their support. Their help changed my life and enabled me to 'show up' as a principal.

Ten years later and with experience in three different schools, I was by then classified as an 'experienced principal'. Our region announced a new position called the network chair. I said to the two female principals sitting next to me in a meeting, 'I would like to do that, but it seems a very big job and I don't know if I can.' They both replied that they would love to help me and to stand by my side in this role. So, with the knowledge that I would get the help I needed from colleagues, I applied for the position and was appointed. I now had the responsibility for leading the network of twenty-seven schools.

Leading a network is not like leading a school. You have to rely on influence and you don't line-manage anyone. There was a voice inside me saying, 'Why do you think you can do this? No one will follow you!' It was so hard keeping this voice quiet and small. The voice never went away, and it would hide and pop up when I least wanted it around.

At first, I spent hours over-planning so that nothing could go wrong. As I started to build trust within the executive team, I realised we would achieve more if everyone's talents were being used, not just mine. I was reminded about my first few months as a principal and how much pleasure others got from helping me in my time of need. I realised that I needed to be able to role-model vulnerability. Once again the voice in my head was saying, 'You are supposed to be an experienced principal – you should know this stuff', but, really, I didn't have to know everything. As a team, we explored our strengths and weaknesses and started to leverage these to achieve our shared goals.

As soon as I started to embrace and consciously use my skills of inclusion, empowering others and providing opportunities for engagement around the work that mattered, we saw a shift in energy and outcome within the network. My invitational style was perceived to be so effective that I stepped out of my own school, helping to lead the network initiative across the whole of Victoria. I worked with school and network leaders across the state for the Bastow Institute of Educational Leadership.

I learned that:

- You are a better leader if you ask for help, and people will follow if they think they can contribute in a meaningful way.

- People are just waiting to help others; it is a way of building connection, and humans want to connect.

- When you step back from trying to be the 'knower', it gives you the opportunity to achieve more, not less.

Actions to take when learning to ask for help:

- Be curious when talking with colleagues and find out what tasks people like doing and what they think they are good at.

- When you are unsure on something, pick up the phone and call a colleague! Be clear about what exactly you need help with.

- Always ring your colleague after the project is done, share with them the outcome and how their help made a difference.

Imperfect leaders create a help-seeking culture

Asking for help as a leader is an effective leadership strategy for all the reasons set out above, but how do we, as leaders, practise and develop help-seeking behaviours? How do we build the skills to express the need for help? By practising reaching out when

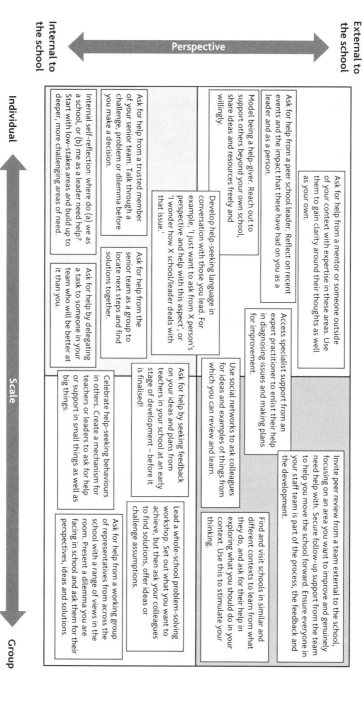

Figure 3.1. Help-seeking matrix

you need help, you can transform the culture of your school towards openness – where asking for help is a sign of an appetite for growth and development rather than a sign of weakness.

In education, we have accidentally perpetuated the notion that teaching, and even school leadership, is a solo sport. From our earliest experiences as trainee teachers, success was achieved when we were able to be left on our own with a class of students (with the door closed!) and when we didn't need help from our mentor any more – we could do it on our own. With students, we teach them the value of learning with others, asking questions, making errors and learning from mistakes; we encourage them to ask for help all the time. In the very best examples of teacher development and leadership development the same principles are applied, and the result is an engrained culture of learning. As imperfect leaders, we need to continue to eradicate the silo mentality and ensure that our teachers, our leaders and our schools are connected to one another in ways that mean we can all ask for help.

For imperfect leaders who want to ask for help more often, Figure 3.1 suggests some examples of help-seeking behaviours.

 ## Prompts for personal reflection

▧ How many of these help-seeking behaviours are evident in your leadership? Would members of your senior leadership team recognise the range of ways that you, as an imperfect leader, seek help within and beyond the school?

▧ Explore whether your help-seeking behaviours include the perspectives of colleagues within your school, as well as whether you are open to external help. Also consider whether you are able to ask for help from a group of people, both within and beyond your school. The latter is the most vulnerable position but can also be the most transformative.

Some leaders we have spoken to confess that when they first engaged in peer review, they tried to ensure that the review team focused only on areas in which the leader thought the school was already strong rather than expose areas of potential weakness. When you are just beginning to engage in peer review, it is understandable that you may feel vulnerable under scrutiny. In fact, focusing on areas of strength can be a powerful way to validate self-evaluation and benchmark practice. However, the real power of invitational leadership and asking for help is when the leader has the courage to admit that they don't have all the answers, and that they know the solution lies in the connections they make with others – within and beyond the school – in the pursuit of better learning and better outcomes for children and young people.

The redwood trees of California offer a helpful analogy which supports this point. David Murphy, former president of the British Psychological Society, shared this in a recent address:

> The coastal redwood is the largest on planet earth, standing at over 400 feet, and also one of the oldest at up to 3,500 years of age. Despite its elevated stature, its roots descend to a relatively shallow depth of about 12 feet, which seems inherently instable. However, the secret of the redwood's success is that its roots grow out to a diameter of 100 feet and are interconnected with those of many other trees. This provides not only stability, but also the opportunity to share water and nutrients between trees. When I visited the forests where they grow naturally, a park ranger told me, to my surprise, that I could have found some in the UK. However, the coastal redwood grown on its own will only grow to a fraction of its usual height, will be pale in colour and is unlikely to live very long. We are all connected and rely on others, just like the redwood trees. It's just that some people don't acknowledge it. (Murphy, 2020)

Prompts for personal reflection

- To what extent are you aware of how easy it is for leaders and teachers to ask for help when they need it and how can you find this out?

- Explore the extent to which your colleagues tend to have a ready-made solution at the start of a conversation compared to asking for the input and help of others.

- What help-seeking behaviours and routines can you employ?

Summary

3

Asking for Help

Asking for help is a powerful and effective leadership strategy, but too often leaders are reluctant to do so because they are concerned it will damage their credibility and undermine their competence. At the heart of imperfect leadership is a complete acceptance that nobody knows all the answers and that we owe it to those we lead to be the best that we can be. We therefore ask for help because it:

- Can develop a sense of collective responsibility.

- Can lead to better decision-making.

- Is more likely to lead to trusting behaviours within the school.

- Enables us to be more resilient or, if we fall down, to get back up again.

Being invitational in our approach also helps us to develop a more fulfilling culture that supports effective collaboration within and across schools.

 ## Exercises to try

- Reflect on your own leadership – what are you good at and where do you want to develop? Seek out a mentor with expertise in an aspect of your leadership that you want to develop. When approaching them, acknowledge their expertise and explain why you want their help. Promise them that if they are willing to mentor you, then you will use the time well and prepare in advance to make the meetings as effective as possible.

- If you have a mentor and value the help you receive, talk openly with colleagues in your school about how having a mentor is benefitting you.

- Reflect on an area within your school where you know that it could be better. Use Figure 3.1 to plan some help-seeking conversations which will support you to find solutions and ways forward.

- Engage in peer-review relationships with other schools. Invite them to review areas of strength and areas where you want their insight to help you and your school to improve.

Chapter 4
Managing Ego and Acknowledging Mistakes

Whenever I climb, I am followed by a dog called ego.

Anon.

Imperfect leaders cultivate a healthy ego.

Being a leader with a healthy ego is important. By ego, we mean someone who has a good level of self-esteem and understands the significance of the role they have as a leader. Sometimes we hear the word ego described in ways that could make you think that it is something to be avoided, but a healthy ego is something that every leader needs to cultivate.

When people take up a leadership role they put on the mantle of leadership. They understand that they are now a leader and accept the fact that they are the person in charge and accountable. Most of us do this with quite a bit of worry but also with some gravitas and with a positive determination to be the best leader we can be.

However, some people find themselves in a leadership role even though deep down they believe that perhaps they shouldn't be a leader at all. They have an ego that is too small. They are neither confident nor resolute. They are overly self-effacing. If you find yourself being led by a leader like this, it can be extremely difficult. Nobody wants to be led by someone who lacks confidence and who is constantly seeking reassurance from their team. Such leaders cannot be challenged easily because they are fragile and go to pieces after even the slightest criticism. Moreover, they don't take tough decisions or see change through.

On the other hand, there are other leaders who, especially after having had some success, not only put on the mantle of leadership but also wear the crown! Their ego becomes overinflated. They start to think they know it all. They talk more and listen less. They start to believe in themselves too much and to drink their own bathwater. Being led by someone with an unhealthily big ego is a nightmare too. You cannot challenge such a leader – you can only tell them what they want to hear, as they think they know best anyway. In the end, this leads to a very top-down, non-distributed leadership model; it fails to empower others or to develop future leaders.

We have both wrestled with this tension in our own leadership. At times in our careers as leaders we have not been very clear in our own minds about what to do; we have lacked the confidence to steer the team and the organisation in the right direction. At other times, when we have had a lot of success, we have become too overconfident and complacent – not welcoming enough challenge and not curious enough about other ways of doing things. We are both at our best as leaders when we have the right balance between confidence and humility; when we are a little scared but not so scared that we become frozen and debilitated; neither overwhelmed nor overbearing. We lead with clarity and decisiveness, but we are constantly thinking about what might go wrong and managing risk. It is a hard line to walk, and we have learned that some self-doubt and fear of failure is a good thing.

 Steve

I used to keep a diary and make entries in it about my leadership issues – how I was feeling, what my hopes and worries were and so on.

In the summer of 2007, I wrote in my diary: 'I have been thinking about my own ability to do the NCSL [National College for School Leadership] job. I seem to remember last year and the year before over the summer holidays I reflected on whether I was up to the job – whether it is just too hard for me. I am thinking this again this summer.'

So, every year I seemed to have self-doubt about my ability to do the job. What I found each year, however, was that once I returned to work after the summer break, my confidence came back and the year ahead went pretty well.

On reflection, I think I would have been a less successful leader if I hadn't been wrestling with some self-doubt each summer.

Table 4.1 outlines some of the characteristics of a healthy ego, alongside what it can look like if it becomes unhealthy.

Table 4.1. The characteristics of an unhealthy and healthy ego

Unhealthy small ego	Healthy ego	Unhealthy big ego
An underdeveloped sense of self-esteem means that you rarely feel happy with yourself and lack confidence.	You are fundamentally happy with yourself, have a good level of self-esteem and are confident in your leadership.	An overinflated sense of self means that you portray yourself as overly self-assured and overly confident.
You hate being in the limelight and try to avoid it because it makes you feel exposed and vulnerable. You shrink into the shadows whenever possible. You may find you push your team around you to fill the gap you have left.	You can enjoy the limelight in situations where you need to be highly visible, but you don't always need it and are satisfied with being unseen and in the background when appropriate. You are able to empower others to lead and know when to step back. You take delight when others are successful and are praised.	You need the limelight, to be centre stage and visible. You dominate with your presence. You don't allow others around you the space to contribute or share the limelight with you. It irritates you if others are seen to be successful.

Unhealthy small ego	Healthy ego	Unhealthy big ego
When people disagree with you, you find it difficult to recover and feel deflated or broken by the challenge and as a result change your mind too often. Alternatively, you create a culture where people don't disagree with you because they know you will react emotionally.	You can handle it when others disagree with you or challenge you, and you are open to changing your mind. You create a culture where colleagues know that you will listen to their perspective and weigh that up alongside other factors.	When people disagree with you, you find ways to disregard their viewpoint, minimise it or make it invalid in some way. Alternatively, you create a culture where people don't disagree with you because they know you will react with anger or be dismissive.
You minimise any praise or thanks you get, deflecting it on to others or disregarding it. You may be in danger of thinking that any success has nothing to do with you.	You can accept praise and thanks from others graciously. You are able to own your achievements and the things you have done well, but are also quick to share the praise and thanks with others who have contributed.	You thrive on what people think about you, and you need their praise and affirmation to feel good about yourself. You sometimes forget to share the credit with others in your team who have contributed and may be in danger of thinking it is all about you.
You are overly sensitive to what people think about you and feel paralysed about making decisions because of how they will be viewed by others.	You care about what people think about you and the decisions you make, but you don't let this paralyse you or stop you from leading. You can make difficult decisions when needed, recognising the range of ways in which they will be viewed by others.	You are not very sensitive to what people think about you. You believe that you are usually right in your actions, irrespective of how they might be viewed by others.

Developing self-efficacy

The concept of self-efficacy is a helpful way of thinking about how to develop a healthy ego. It was first defined by Albert Bandura in 1977. It can be understood as a person's belief in their ability to succeed in any given situation. Developing and nurturing a robust and healthy ego requires us to have a strong belief in ourselves as leaders. In practice, this looks like leaders who are reflective, resilient and courageous; leaders who create a culture of openness and honesty; leaders who learn from mistakes and can embrace failure whilst remaining persistent and focused.

In the case study that follows, Liz Robinson describes how she had to wrestle with her own ego as she unpicked a school improvement challenge in her school. But she also exemplifies what self-efficacy looks like in practice. She acknowledges the fears she had along the way and the pressure she felt, as well as how she and her team reflected together and learned how to create a more sustainable culture of improvement and excellence.

 ## Case study

Liz Robinson, co-director, Big Education

I was head teacher and then co-head teacher at Surrey Square Primary School from 2006 to 2018. The school serves a complex and materially disadvantaged community in South-East London. I began as head teacher of the junior school (7–11-year-olds) and led the school through a period of transformation. I then took on the infant school (3–7-year-olds) and amalgamated the two to form a primary school. Shortly after this, I became pregnant with my first child. Values were the driver of my approach to school improvement – my belief in equity, high expectations and a person-centred approach to learning. The mission of the school is 'Personal and academic excellence, everyone, every day'.

When I returned from my first maternity leave, I was struck by how quickly some of the systems, processes and behaviours – things that I thought were embedded – had actually slipped, and the education and culture was suffering. The junior school had previously been judged outstanding by Ofsted, and I felt a huge weight of pressure and expectation on me to achieve this same judgement with the newly formed primary school. I had also been fast-tracked in my leadership career and became a head teacher in my twenties. I knew that there were lots of eyes watching me – and not all of them wanted me to succeed.

This was a deeply challenging time for me, as I had always believed that a mark of great leadership is the ability to walk away and for everything to continue in your absence. I had to engage in thorough reflection about what had happened and what we could do to sort it out.

What became clear was that this was an issue of responsibility or, more accurately, the lack of a deep feeling in all staff members of being responsible for the standards of the school. I had to reflect on the fact that the deputy (who was on maternity leave at the same time) and I had 'held' too much of that – we were somehow the custodians of excellence for the school.

Managing my own feelings of failure (how could this have happened?), anxiety (do I know how to fix this?) and insecurity (I'm not as good at this as I thought I was), alongside being a sleep-deprived new mum to baby Ella, was really hard. There was a huge amount of soul-searching as we looked to find a way to re-establish the culture of self-motivation and put things right. It had to start with deep reflection on my own behaviour and how this had (inadvertently) played a role in creating an inconsistent sense of responsibility in the staff body. I had been leading with more of a top-down management approach than I thought I had; my leadership and oversight was still very much relied upon as a driver within the school.

I worked with the senior team, looking at our own behaviours and approaches first and then thinking about how best to work with the rest of the team. Our approach included:

▪ **A new message to the team.** Our key insight was around the need to restate our vision of excellence. Some things had slipped and we needed to make it clear that that was not okay with us. We needed to make our expectations and vision for the school explicitly clear to everyone again. Alongside that was the message that it is everyone's responsibility to make the school great. We accepted that we had held that overall sense of responsibility too much ourselves, and this was a new start. The expectation was that every staff member needed to develop the same burning sense of responsibility that we both had.

Clarifying our vision. Our values were very established in the school, but we did not have an overarching vision statement. We worked on that. Through many hours of debate, we arrived on the current statement – 'Personal and academic excellence, everyone, every day' – heavily influenced by these experiences and emphasising the role of every person to make this a reality.

Codifying the behaviours we wanted to see. Working as a leadership team, we developed the model below, which names and describes the types of behaviours we were seeing and those we wanted to support the team to move towards. This was a powerful way of giving a road map and making explicit the different approaches we wanted to support – approaches which would build capacity. Breaking it down into stages enabled people to learn and to be coached above their responsibilities, and the model is still used in school today.

How to build capacity – a model from Surrey Square	
Level 5	Whole-school strategy change
Level 4	Coaching/facilitating others – challenge and praise
Level 3	Setting clear expectations and responsibilities with delegated authority
Level 2	Telling someone else to do it and following up/checking
Level 1	Doing it yourself
Level 0.5	Moaning/feeling frustrated and doing nothing
Level 0	Doing nothing and forgetting about it

Pride

Trust

Capacity

Sustain

There was a release of energy as people got back in touch with their personal responsibility and the sense of empowerment that comes with that. It was a reset moment, and the organisation moved into a period of rapid improvement and growth.

This process provided a great learning opportunity for us as leaders, reflecting on the need to keep revisiting our core ideas and purpose on a regular basis with the whole team. I see the school as being in a state of dynamic equilibrium; in order to even maintain our practice, let alone improve it, we must put in a huge amount of positive energy. This connects to the concept of entropy – the process through which every organism decays or the 'gradual decline into disorder'.[1] As leaders, the challenge, then, is to find ways to counter this tendency and to keep all members of the team connected with their sense of personal responsibility to maintain and improve their practice every single day.

For me, personally, it helped me to shift my own concept of leadership and what success looks like. Our accountability system in England is exceptionally high stakes; the pressure it puts on you as a leader is extreme. As someone who was driven by achievement and success, I was trapped in a sense of that mattering above all else. This period was critical in re-evaluating what really mattered to me and developing my own more nuanced understanding of excellence in school leadership, deeply rooted in an understanding that systemic, holistic approaches to leadership are the only way to create really sustainable change.

There are a number of ways we can increase our self-efficacy:

- **Experience and reflect on success.** You have heard the phrase 'success breeds success' and there is some truth in this. Succeeding at a task impacts on the way we think about ourselves – we gain a sense of mastery and confidence that we can achieve similar results again. To build a healthy ego, we need to allow ourselves to be nourished by the things that we do well and where we have had successes. In addition, where we fail, we need to accept that failure positively and develop

---

1   See https://www.lexico.com/definition/entropy.

resilience. Leaders who succeed after overcoming an obstacle or recovering from a failure develop a stronger sense of self-efficacy.

- **Learn from others.** We can develop self-efficacy by learning from and listening to other leaders who have achieved success in similar circumstances – people to whom we can relate. This is why we believe that having mentors and role models is so important. Our sense of being able to succeed is influenced by other people's achievements – we need to allow ourselves to be encouraged and motivated.

- **Goal-setting.** One practical way to develop self-efficacy is to set goals and articulate our intentions. Low self-efficacy can make us doubt our abilities or believe that the tasks ahead are more difficult than they are. One way to generate and sustain self-efficacy is to set simple goals, with manageable steps to achieving them, and then approach them one by one. By doing this, we can celebrate our small successes and our goals become more achievable and accessible. For example, imagine your ultimate goal is to run a marathon; by setting interim goals for what you can achieve each week as you build your stamina and confidence, your sense of self-efficacy and belief in yourself will grow week on week. Being clear about what we are intending to achieve really helps us attend to ourselves as leaders and to what we are committing.

- **Treat setbacks, mistakes and failures as opportunities for growth.** Sometimes a small knock-back can lead us to believe that complete failure is inevitable and fatal. To nurture self-efficacy, keep focused on the ultimate goal and accept that challenges and failures along the way are inevitable. We must continue to believe in ourselves and our abilities and look for the opportunities for learning which will help us to recover our sense of agency.

When leaders forget they are imperfect

In 2016, a headline appeared in the *TES*: 'Charting the downfall of the "famous five" superheads' (Vaughan, 2016). The story was about five school head teachers in England who had achieved great success, had been praised by the education minister at the time and were described as heroes. They had become well-known in education circles and had been involved in advising government officials and ministers on policy issues. All five of these superheads lost their jobs; four were banned from ever teaching again and one of the five actually went to prison.

What this exemplifies is that there are some leaders who achieve a level of success and then forget that they are imperfect. They believe in themselves so much that they think the rules somehow don't apply to them. Their egos are out of control. A clinical study by Daniel Sankowsky (1995) illustrates that when charisma overlaps with narcissism, leaders tend to abuse their power and take advantage of their followers. That is why it is so important to be mindful that we are all imperfect leaders.

 ## Marie-Claire

A few years ago, I was working and leading within a collaborative partnership of system leaders (national leaders of education (NLEs)) who had come together to deliver support and professional development to schools in our local area. We had regular meetings together to plan and talk about our work and the impact we were having. As a relatively new NLE, I found these meetings extremely challenging. At times I felt intimidated by the self-confidence – and the egos – of some colleagues in the room.

On one occasion, I was invited by one of the NLEs to meet him in his head office to 'talk'. I knew from the tone of the recent meetings that he had concerns about some of the decisions I had made as chair of the partnership and that he wanted more say and more transparency. With trepidation I agreed to meet him.

In preparing for the meeting, I could see that there were a number of different approaches I could take. He was an extremely impressive man and led a group of successful schools. Should I be deferential, subservient and apologetic? Should I bolster my own ego and approach it with absolute self-assuredness and confidence in the decisions I had made? Should I take a defensive posture and prepare to justify and prove myself, with a rationale and arguments backing up my position? My ego was fluctuating between two extremes of unhealthiness. I decided that what I needed to do first was to try and see the situation through his eyes and understand his drivers and motivations. Stephen Covey (2020, p. 28) says, 'We see the world not as *it is*, but as *we are*,' so how did he see the world and why was that different from how I saw the world?

I formulated a list of questions that I wanted to ask him to get under the skin of who he was, what he was about and how he saw the world. I also prepared some paperwork in advance, ready to pull out and share to demonstrate complete transparency, explaining the processes we had gone through to reach decisions.

The meeting went well. He showed me around his office, and I got a sense of the detailed grasp he had of his schools. He had a huge whiteboard on one wall detailing every employee and where he was planning to deploy them the following year. Listening to him, I could hear his ambition for the children and young people in his care and his eye for quality. Seeing him in his own context, with pictures of his family on the wall, was powerful. I began to see the person behind the 'challenge' and began to get a sense of what it was that made him tick. He was exceptionally proud of all he had achieved during his long career, and his challenge to our partnership was coming from a desire for more detail and, ultimately, for his organisation to play a bigger part in the work.

Over the following years I built a good relationship with him and his organisation, and when he retired I was pleased to make a speech noting publicly that the meeting we'd had in his office was a significant learning point for me in managing my own ego when dealing with criticism. Through this experience, I learned to navigate relationships like this one with curiosity, openness and a quiet self-confidence, as opposed to being either too defensive or too deferential. Being open to challenge but also being clear about my position. I learned that I needed to keep my own ego in balance – not too strong but not absent either.

As leaders in education, we are immersed in the work of learning and development as we seek to see the children and young people for whom we are responsible flourish. We are also committed to improving the practice of the teachers and leaders in our schools. All of this is grounded in a belief that change is possible and that everyone in our organisation should be on a journey to become a better version of themselves. When we give students feedback on their work or teachers feedback on the learning happening in their lessons, we should be giving feedback for growth.

However, we should be mindful that when we give feedback to our colleagues it can be received as criticism and can challenge their sense of self-esteem or ego. We sometimes see this in students too, when they react badly to correction. As imperfect leaders, we have to work hard to create a culture where we give feedback for growth and where we help one another to develop a healthy ego in response to advice. One of the ways we can do this is by sharing how the feedback we have received as leaders has helped us to become better leaders and to make better decisions.

The case study below from Stef Edwards illustrates an easy mistake that we can make as leaders. Occasionally, we can become so enthusiastic about something, so convinced about the merit of our own ideas and plans, that we fail to truly listen to those around us. Stef describes a significant shift in her own imperfect leadership as she reflects on the power of listening, curiosity and feedback. She describes her own sense of imposter syndrome which can often get in the way of developing a healthy ego.

 ## Case study

Stef Edwards, trust leader, Learn Academies Trust, Leicestershire, England

I embarked on headship in 2006. I left a job as a part-time class teacher in a tiny village school in 2003 to work as a primary literacy strategy consultant, advising schools about primary English and delivering training for teachers. Three years later, I returned to the fray as the teaching head of a small school. Armed with a national school leadership qualification, I was the embodiment of imposter syndrome but with an enormous capacity for learning from mistakes. This was just as well because I made lots of them.

The experience I had of school improvement was founded on leadership of professional learning, mostly about reading, writing, grammar and spelling. I was convinced that this was the way forward. My intentions were honourable, but I do have a tendency to be a bit convinced of my own righteousness. I fall into the trap of thinking everyone understands what is in my head and how I arrived at my surely very annoying strong convictions. This is a battle I wage to this day. Me, myself and I often have to have stern words.

When I heard about Lesson Study from Dr Peter Dudley and Professor David Pedder at a local professional development network meeting, I was completely sold.[2] I dreamed about the possibilities and potential for teachers' professional learning on my way home in the car. I waxed lyrical (in my head) about the scope for collaboration, teacher agency, research engagement and knowledge mobilisation. I made amazing PowerPoint slides and planned an incisive and persuasive staff meeting. I wrote a marvellous proposal for the school governors. I applied for funding all over the place and, hey presto, we were off within three to four months.

But it didn't work out the way I thought it would. It just didn't seem to inspire the same enthusiasm from all the teachers, especially when I tried to persuade colleagues in other schools to join in. I got funding for inter-school Lesson Study, and I patted myself on the back for being innovative and forward-thinking. But, actually, some teachers (in other schools, not mine – the teachers in my school were far too kind) said tricky things like, 'It's a complete waste of time.'

Then one day, Professor Pedder came to interview me for a research project about developing great pedagogy. Before he left, he asked me how Lesson Study was going. I painted a rose-tinted picture – mainly because, at that time, I didn't grasp quite how poorly it was going. I was just thrilled it was going at all. He tapped his finger on one of the Lesson Study posters I had shown him and said, 'There's a rich seam of evidence for a doctorate here …'

Those eleven words planted a seed that took about two years to germinate. In 2013 I started an EdD studying the leadership practices which promote and sustain effective Lesson Study. I still haven't finished at the time of writing. I have taken time off to establish and lead a charitable schools trust, and lately there has been the pandemic. It has been very hard, and continues to be hard, but it has nurtured the most valuable learning of my career. The process of enquiry has taught me as much about leadership as all the literature I read for my literature review. It has taught me how much I assumed I knew, when I actually knew very little.

---

2   See https://lessonstudy.co.uk. See also Dudley (2014).

I started out knowing I had a problem with Lesson Study. Preparing my research proposal and drafting my thesis took me through the research enquiry process. I had to define my problem. What precisely was it that I didn't understand enough about? I had to find out – *really* find out – what was already known about that problem. I read research literature that confirmed all my biases and much that made me squirm. I had to work out how to ask the right enquiry questions. I had to work out how to find answers and how to be confident that the answers would be useful and credible. I collected data. I had to learn how best to analyse it. Then I had to analyse it. Again. And again. And again. Until I started to knit some clarity out of my big bag of fog.

Sometimes, the best fog-knitting happens whilst you are asleep, or out walking, or ironing. Sometimes, trying too hard to knit fog too fast leads to dropped stitches. There is a wonderful feeling of epiphany when the fog clears. Strands of something you have been tussling with suddenly crystallise into a newer and hopefully wiser thought.

Interviewing teachers and leaders set the scene for this particular epiphany. Together they held solutions to the problems with our Lesson Study implementation. They were the wise crowd. I just needed to ask them to talk to me and then to listen to them. I made the shift from thinking, 'How could you think that?' to 'Why do you think that?' I grew a little less righteous and much more curious.

Trawling through teachers' and leaders' interview transcripts and acres of field note fragments was agony and ecstasy. Agony because it has taken so long. Ecstasy because it forced me to listen, *really* listen, to their voices, over and over again.

I learned a lot about leading unsuccessful and successful Lesson Study. I learned that I had been completely deluded ever to have thought we could do it after one forty-five-minute presentation at a network event. I learned about the wisdom of crowds. I learned to listen, *really* listen, to lots of different people and perspectives. I learned that to be genuinely curious, you have to ask first and then be the last to speak. I learned about the power of authentic enquiry, of curiosity, when you want to improve something. I learned that when I grow up, I want to be wise.

Practical ways to help you develop a healthy ego

So, how do you develop and maintain a healthy ego? Here are some practical tips:

- Practise active listening. Take the time to listen to others by being fully present and engaged in the conversation (as opposed to predicting what they are going to say next or planning what you are going to say when they stop talking). Someone with a healthy ego gives others the space to speak. They don't need to repeat what has been said already or have the last word. Instead, imperfect leaders build on what others have said, co-create solutions and welcome different ideas.

- Create a culture where it is normal for leaders in the organisation to ask for feedback from one another. For example, ask members of your senior leadership team to regularly feed back to one another (in pairs) the answers to these questions:

  » When do you see me at my best as a leader, and how does that help you?

  » When have I limited you, held you back or got in your way?

  » What do you need me to do better/more of?

  » What do you think I need to pay more attention to?

- Find mentors who are further along the leadership journey than you and listen to them talk about what they are achieving and learning, but also ask them about times when they have got it wrong or made a mistake. Allow that to give you new perspectives on your own leadership context and achievements. Be encouraged by their successes and inspired about your own leadership.

- Keep a journal and note down the things you are proud of – the things you think you have done well each week. Allow yourself to feel good about what you have achieved and your successes as a leader.

- Discuss with trusted colleagues the mistakes you have made and what you have learned by reflecting and putting them right.

- Reflect regularly on what you think you are doing well and where you want to develop and improve your leadership skill; hold both in balance.

▦ Express gratitude for the people around you who contribute to the things you view as successful. Acknowledge their role and thank them.

 ## Prompts for personal reflection

▦ Who are the mentors and role models around you to whom you can look as an encouragement and support in navigating both your successes and your failures? Cultivate trusting relationships where you can explore what you are learning as a leader.

▦ How open are you to feedback? Have you got a default response (defensive, overly sensitive, angry)? How do you manage others who may react in this way when you give them feedback?

Imperfect leaders admit their mistakes

There is an important distinction to be noted between the mistakes leaders make in relation to a task that has gone wrong or not been done and mistakes that are relational. Relational mistakes take place between the leader and other people in the organisation – for example, it might be a poorly managed interaction with a team member, neglecting to ask for input or involvement, not doing what you said you would do or forgetting to recognise someone's contribution. Research by Hetrick et al. (2021, p. 30) found that 'Leaders are more likely to apologize for task mistakes and are more likely to justify their relationship mistakes, rather than admit wrongdoing for them.' This is a challenge for leaders because relational mistakes undermine trust and integrity. Imperfect leaders need to be ready to admit when they have made a relational mistake and quick to apologise and rebuild trust. As leaders, we must be careful when constructing an apology, so that the tone and language we use improves the relationships we have with our colleagues.

Recognising and acknowledging a mistake is an important leadership skill. It is much easier to recognise and admit you have got things wrong when you are looking back months or years later, especially if you are no longer in the same role. For example, political memoirs are far more likely to include admissions of mistakes in the past that were never acknowledged at the time. Apologising years later is important and can mean a lot, but by then it is usually much harder to rectify what went wrong. The really tough leadership skill is acknowledging a mistake at the time and before it is too late, doing something about it.

Some leaders find it impossible to say sorry and, worse still, they even seek to blame others for their mistake. Acknowledging responsibility is key here. Saying: 'I'm sorry that you feel upset about ...' doesn't fool anyone. They know that you haven't really apologised. When it comes to an apology, the most important component is an acknowledgement of responsibility. Imperfect leaders are prepared to say when something is their fault and to own the mistake they have made. People will forgive leaders who make mistakes from time to time and admit to them, but they hate a cover-up or a blame culture.

Research also shows that when leaders give a sincere apology, the people who work for them report higher levels of trust in leadership and organisational commitment, as well as levels of forgiveness, than leaders who are viewed as being insincere or don't apologise at all (Basford et al., 2014). Imperfect leaders don't make 'sorry' the hardest word.

When planning an apology, consider developing a recovery strategy:

- Plan what you are going to say in advance, looking out for the ways you might be tempted to justify or minimise the mistake.

- Think about and articulate what you should have done differently or what you are going to do now to put it right.

- Acknowledge the impact of the error and any pain or upset that it has caused.

- Anticipate how the person might react and think about how you will respond if they accept your apology and how you will respond if they don't.

Steve

Many years ago, I led an assessment team in a local education authority in the North of England. We devised an accreditation system for secondary schools in the local authority to quality assure their assessment procedures. We aimed to set the bar high so that not all schools would meet the criteria, and therefore some would not be fully accredited in the first year.

In the end, we set the bar far too high and no schools met the criteria. Even the schools with very good practice were not accredited. This was a big error on my part. Some members of my team were worried that the whole team would be disbanded as a result. After reflecting upon what had happened, I went to a meeting of all the secondary head teachers and personally apologised to them for what had happened. I took full responsibility and promised them that I would put it right for the following year.

There is no doubt in my mind (and this was confirmed through conversations with some of the head teachers later) that my credibility as a leader went up rather than down as a result. It was important that I acknowledged the mistake, took full responsibility for it, promised to put it right and then put it right.

There are two important caveats about the value of acknowledging mistakes as a leader:

1.   It is harder to admit mistakes to people you don't trust. If you think that individuals are out to get you, it is harder to make yourself vulnerable. That is why building the right culture within the organisation is so important. It is also one of the reasons why so few politicians apologise for anything.

2.   If we admit mistakes and then put them right, we will gain credibility; but if we admit them and then mess up again on the same issue, it will damage our credibility. People who repeatedly make mistakes on the same kind of issue make poor leaders. Good leaders are imperfect but they are also restless learners, and they grow and improve in their leadership, getting better all the time (see Chapter 6).

Taking responsibility for the mistakes of your team

We have an important role to play as leaders in holding members of our team to account for their actions and their impact. It is a key aspect of leadership. It is our job to help our colleagues make good decisions, to give them space to take risks and to challenge them to be the best they can be. It is true that if we want to get the best out of our teams, then our colleagues need to feel able to take risks, which may lead to some mistakes along the way. In taking risks, they need to know that we are watching their back, guiding them and protecting them. They need to know how mistakes will be handled and feel safe to try new things within the agreed parameters.

As imperfect leaders, we believe it is vital to create a culture where, when mistakes are made, they are talked about openly (and privately), with an emphasis on learning from the experience as well as putting things right and avoiding making the same error in the future. There needs to be clear and robust accountability to avoid repeated errors, complacency, inefficiency or persistent underperformance. Of course, if a colleague makes a serious mistake there may be policies that need to be followed and there could be consequences, but if they are acting within policy, under our direction and overall authority, then if it goes wrong we need to be seen to be taking public responsibility.

We know that if a sports manager starts publicly blaming their team for a poor performance, there is something going badly wrong with the culture and the leadership. When mistakes happen in our organisations, as they inevitably will, colleagues in our team need to know that we won't hang them out to dry in front of the staff team, parents or governors. We will own the mistake with them and help to put it right.

Occasionally, when someone in our team makes a mistake, we need to look at the big picture and understand why it was made before acting. We understand that not all mistakes are the result of bad intentions or a deliberate error. The response to any mistake must be proportionate and consider the precise circumstances and the broader picture.

Steve

When I was a director of education in a local education authority, I managed two very talented assistant directors who were both relatively new to the authority and to their senior role. In their enthusiasm and commitment to make an impact, they had both failed to follow procurement rules. Their motives had been completely honourable and the outcomes from their actions were entirely positive, but they had (unknowingly) failed to follow due procedure.

The procurement guidance was written down in a manual that they had received, but it wasn't something that had been drawn to their attention. When the director of finance discovered that there had been a breach of the procurement rules, he commenced an investigation. He was minded to take disciplinary action against both of them. In my view, this would have been unnecessary under the circumstances and would have damaged not only their morale but that of the whole team. In spite of my objections, the director of finance and the chief executive insisted on taking disciplinary action against them.

After much reflection, I concluded – and this is the key point – that my failure to proactively bring the procurement procedures to the attention of the two assistant directors was the main mistake. So, I managed to persuade the chief executive to take disciplinary action against me instead. I argued that I was the accountable officer overall and I had not ensured that my colleagues were aware of what was expected of them, and therefore I should be the one to be disciplined. I received a formal written warning.

It was one of the best decisions that I ever made as a leader. My two colleagues went on to do transformational work for the children and young people in the area, loyalty and trust between the three of us was enhanced even further, and the formal warning was only on my record for three years.

Prompts for personal reflection

- How easy do you find it to say sorry? When was the last time you said sorry in a genuine and authentic way? What impact did your apology have?

- How do you manage the mistakes of people in your team?

A note on gender and ego: it would be amiss not to mention that in our experience there are certain gender stereotypes and unconscious biases which have an influence on both the theme of asking for help (Chapter 3) and this chapter, managing ego and admitting mistakes.

 ## Marie-Claire

Many female leaders (including myself from time to time) suffer from imposter syndrome, have too small an ego and lack confidence in their abilities. (I am sure there are male leaders who suffer from this too, but in my experience it is more common amongst women.) The way this manifests itself for me is a fear that I will be misjudged and misunderstood for displaying my ego or acting with confidence in myself and what I think I can achieve. So, I downplay myself, I am overly self-deprecating at times and I regularly deflect any praise that comes my way for fear that I will be judged as being egotistical. For men there is often a different challenge. Rosette et al. (2015) suggest that some male leaders find it difficult to ask for help for fear that their skills and abilities as leaders may be questioned and perceptions of their male gender role impaired. Imperfect leadership requires us to have a balance in our leadership, which means we are able to ask for help, admit mistakes and simultaneously maintain a healthy ego and confidence in ourselves.

Prompt for personal reflection

Does this resonate with you? How can you create a climate in your school or organisation where asking for help is not a gender-specific phenomenon?

Summary

Managing Ego

and Acknowledging Mistakes

If we have an imperfect leadership mindset:

- We are not afraid of admitting mistakes.

- We are open to learning and open to hearing feedback.

- We are quick to say sorry when it is the right thing to do.

- We hold ourselves in good esteem and actively cultivate a healthy ego – not too small and not too big.

Exercises to try

Using Table 4.1, reflect on any statements about the characteristics of an unhealthy and healthy ego which resonate with you.

- Think of times when you have acted in a way which demonstrates a healthy ego and reflect on the impact that had on those around you, as well as on you. How did you feel? How did you make others feel?

- Reflect on the times when you have been on the receiving end of someone acting with an unhealthy ego. How did you feel? How did it make others feel?

- Choose one statement from the healthy ego column which you would like to strengthen, and plan what you are going to say and do to demonstrate this to others.

Chapter 5
Making Public Promises

Never make a promise in haste.

Mahatma Gandhi

Imperfect leaders know how and when to make public promises.

Around the world, we are used to hearing politicians announce their election promises to the constituents they hope to serve. Despite these public promises, in the UK (as well as in other democracies) political trust is low and distrust is growing (Foa et al., 2020). It seems not everyone believes that politicians keep their commitments once elected. Leading in education is a different arena, but the link between making public promises and maintaining trust is important. Leaders with an imperfect leadership mindset learn how and when to make public promises: they only make them after careful consideration and they understand the purpose of making this kind of declaration.

What do we mean by public promises?

Specifically, we mean a promise which is made public in some way about our leadership, our values, the way in which we will behave and the approaches we will take as a leader – that is, a public declaration about our own behaviour, not a promise for organisational success (or an election-style pledge). There are often too many variables for leaders to be able to declare with any certainty that their school will achieve certain targets. Nor is it right to make a public promise about other people's behaviour. Making public promises is about personal commitment, not organisational commitment – it is a public social contract.

Why make public promises?

Making public promises is one way to help us stay true as a leader and to lead in the way we want to lead

As imperfect leaders, we know that we sometimes get it wrong. We often know the right action or decision to take, but we are also aware that, when the pressures mount and other priorities come rushing in, we may lose sight of what really matters. We understand that leadership is very hard and that whilst having high ideals and good strategic plans are important, they are not enough. Making public promises is one way of helping leaders who know they are imperfect to do what really matters.

Making public promises is a strategy first and foremost to help us. It is particularly powerful when we publicly commit to something we know that we will find hard, but we also know that it will make the school or organisation we lead a better place to learn and work. Once a public promise is made, it is much harder to conveniently forget what we said we would do, or to recall only a few conditions of a promise, or even to back out entirely. There is a healthy element of peer pressure, which, in this context, can be a good thing. It helps us to stay focused on what we have agreed to do. Psychologists have found that most people strive to keep that promise, and with higher levels of personal motivation and commitment (Knox and Inkster, 1968). After all, their reputation for competence and trustworthiness is on the line.

Promises made, monitored and completed in public feel high stakes; therefore, we should give serious consideration to what promises we do make. We should only make public declarations about things that we know are very important for us to achieve as leaders – ambitions that are achievable but also meaningful and significant. It is also important that the promise is made voluntarily and is therefore genuine. As a result, we will be instinctively motivated to take responsibility for keeping that promise. As Rachel Kitley says in her case study that follows, making public promises introduces 'a level of accountability which can be far more powerful than the accountability you feel to an external body, because you commit emotionally and wholeheartedly to a personal promise.'

🔍 Case study

Rachel Kitley, principal, Cowes Enterprise College, Isle of Wight, England

When I began my headship at Cowes Enterprise College, a secondary academy on the Isle of Wight, I stepped into a very challenging scenario – the school had been judged inadequate by Ofsted and was in special measures. The community reputation was poor, staff morale was low and the school's new sponsor, Ormiston Academies Trust, had only just taken on the school. There had been numerous short-stay head teachers across a sustained period of over seven years, and a couple of years earlier the entire student body had gone on strike, essentially about a lack of trust in the school leadership. This issue had been reported in the national media.

During my first week, a member of staff (and union rep) came unannounced into my office and said, with no preamble, 'We're not going to do a thing you want us to do because you'll be gone by Christmas.'

I needed people to believe in me as their new head teacher quickly, and I had to build immediate trust across all stakeholders if I was to achieve any worthwhile change. I made a public promise to all stakeholders that I would stay as the principal, earn their trust, be resilient and make the school everything it could be, at pace. I promised the regional schools commissioner, a senior education official at the Department for Education, that I would be the 'arm of the community'. I promised the students that I would put them at the centre of every decision I made. And I promised my own family that we would never regret relocating from London to the local community or moving the children from an outstanding London school to join what was then a special measures school. I promised the community that if the school was going to be good enough for my own children very quickly, then it would be good enough for everyone's children too. I managed to fast-track a year's worth of trust-building into one term, and when we had an Ofsted inspection just three weeks into my headship, I believe I was also able to instil trust in the promise of my future headship in the inspectors.

What key ingredients enabled me to condense gaining trust and credibility into such a short space of time? I believe I am a very warm, sincere and genuine person – what you see is what you get. I don't have frills. I think that this comes across loud and clear when anyone interacts with me; they pick up on my characteristics straight away and so are willing to take a chance on me. If you couple all this with the fact that I promised and talked out loud to staff, students, parents/carers and the community on numerous occasions during my first term, then it is clear that I made myself wholly available for people to believe in me and my key messages.

I spent time building relationships. I listened. I was open, honest and worked to create a sense of team. I focused on culture and ethos in every moment of the day – for instance, being pleasantly uncompromising in resisting pressure from people who believed they were entitled to special privileges. I began to win trust through promises; a huge breakthrough was when one influential parent said to me, 'I'll give you a try.' I showed calm, decisive, child-centred leadership, modelling expectations in every conversation I had. First-term quick-fixes were about valuing people – for instance, introducing free tea/coffee to the staffroom, a weekly parent surgery and sending personally written thank-you cards. I was eternally optimistic but also realistic about where we were.

I am now in my fourth year as head teacher. We have a very strong reputation in the community and are hugely oversubscribed, showing that the community has real faith in the school. I believe that I have met those public promises (of course, we have much more to do and I continue to make promises). We are now rated good by Ofsted, our GCSE exam results are the best on the island and more than half of our sixth-form students are applying to Russell Group universities or to study medicine.

Making public promises can be a really effective thing for an imperfect leader to do. They provide a level of accountability which can be far more powerful than the accountability you feel to an external body because you commit emotionally and wholeheartedly to a personal promise. The public nature of a promise means others will believe in it too. A promise is simple and therefore can also help to keep something complex like the management of change simple. The school's strength can come from the head teacher without you being a 'hero head' but by making authentic, honest pledges. I also know that you can get nowhere on your own. I have had great support from the whole staff team, from parents, from students, the governors and from the leadership of Ormiston Academies Trust.

It is easy to make promises, of course, but it also needs extraordinary levels of resilience to deliver on them, and this comes from knowing yourself well and having good support networks. Most of all, you need to be totally committed to your promises at a moral purpose level.

 Steve

Just before I started my role as CEO of the National College for School Leadership, I made a speech at a large conference. In this speech I made a very important public commitment: I declared that I would personally telephone the chair of each secondary head teachers' group, each primary head teachers' group and each special head teachers' group in each local education authority, along with other key stakeholders, to ask them for advice as to what I should do as the new CEO and to invite them all to attend one of nine regional conferences to discuss the future of the National College. As there were 150 local education authorities, I was publicly committing myself to make about 500 telephone calls to school head teachers within the first few months of being in the role.

I had a very tough time trying to make those 500 phone calls. I needed to do them in the space of ten weeks, which meant that on average I needed to make ten phone calls per day for fifty consecutive working days. If I hadn't made a public commitment to do this, I probably would have given up. I had no idea how hard it was going to be.

When I was the director of education in Knowsley, if I telephoned a school in Knowsley then the head teacher invariably took the call. But now that I was telephoning schools all over the country, often the school office thought that I was trying to sell something and refused to put me through. I often had to call back two or three times to actually get to speak to the head teacher. But I made all those calls myself – every single one – and it turned out to be one of the most effective things I did as CEO of the National College. Some head teachers never forgot that I had called them personally to listen to their views, and the message soon spread in every area that the new CEO of the National College wanted to listen to the voice of school leaders.

I learned from this, and from my experiences later, that making public commitments can sometimes be risky, but it can also keep you on track and help to make sure that you do the right thing when you are under pressure.

Making public promises invites relational accountability

In Rwanda, the tribal chiefs and leaders used to make a public *Imihigo* or 'vow to deliver'. They would state publicly in front of their tribe what their goals were and declare that they were determined to overcome any possible challenges that arose in achieving those goals. This approach helped to develop a sense of trust and of personal and collective accountability between the tribal chief and the tribe. It is interesting that this practice continues in Rwanda amongst all senior leaders in the public sector. If you are, for example, the new CEO of a hospital, you will be expected to hold a meeting of all staff to set out your goals and make a public promise about what the staff can expect from you as CEO.

As imperfect leaders, we know that once a public promise is made, we are deliberately opening ourselves up to challenge and to being held publicly accountable for our actions and behaviours. This is why making public promises is so closely linked to building trust and personal accountability. Once we make a public promise, we must be prepared to revisit, reflect and share our progress towards that promise publicly as well.

 Steve

In 2012, I made the decision to do the Great North Run. This is a half marathon in Newcastle upon Tyne. I knew that if I was going to complete the race, I would need to get fit and get up very early on many mornings in order to go running. This was a real effort for me and I struggled. I had a very demanding job at the time, which was taking up huge amounts of my time and energy. I felt that in order to incentivise me to do the half marathon and the necessary training, I needed a moral purpose. So, I decided to run in aid of Macmillan Cancer Support – a great charity. However, even with this moral purpose as an incentive, it still wasn't enough to get me up early and do the training. What really made the difference for me was that I told all my friends and colleagues that I was going to do the Great North Run. Having made a public declaration, it would have been unthinkable for me to have gone back on it.

Making public promises supports learning, growth and changes behaviour

When we make a public commitment to do something, our motivation increases. One of the reasons that weight loss programmes like Weight Watchers or Slimming World work is because of the requirement to state publicly how much weight you want to commit to losing in the following week. As a result, there is a very transparent evaluation on a weekly basis! There is a healthy level of peer pressure which actually incentivises commitment to the weight loss plan.

Dylan Wiliam takes this concept and applies it to professional development strategies in schools. He calls it 'supportive accountability':

> The model that I think would be implementable at scale is to establish monthly workshops … so at the end of each meeting each participant promises her or his colleagues about what they are going to try out during the coming month. At the next meeting, everyone (everyone!) comes back to report on how it went. Repeatedly, we've had teachers comment on how silly they felt initially writing down their promise for the group, but expressing surprise that it does actually work. It's like Weight Watchers – promising to try something out and then being held accountable at the end of that process. It's what makes you prioritise developing your practice over all the other things that everybody tells you are priorities in school as well. (Wiliam, 2006)

Professional learning communities (PLCs) is one way that this approach has been systematised with a consistent focus on teacher development. PLCs work best when teachers make a public commitment to a group of peers about what they intend to improve in their practice using learning from evidence and research. For example, a commitment made might be the following:

- I will focus on the following students ... who currently have the following needs ...

- If I am successful in meeting their needs, instead of seeing ... I will see ... in my lesson and in their work.

The critical part is that they are then given the opportunity for routine reflection on progress and impact. The international evidence about the impact of PLCs is clear: this approach, when done well, can have a profound impact on improving teacher practice (Stoll et al., 2006). Imperfect leaders seek out opportunities to reflect and learn from the evidence and research about leadership, and they build a professional learning community which helps them to reflect on their public promises and grow and develop as leaders.

Making public promises influences those we lead

A public promise rarely occurs in isolation, and it has a ripple effect on those we lead. When we make a public promise, we must recognise that we have an influence on those around us and there is power in what we say. As imperfect leaders, we know that in order to deliver on a public promise we may need to solicit and oversee a network of supporting commitments from colleagues to help us keep on track and deliver what we have promised. It is also important to remember that members of our team will pay very close attention to what we promise, and those closest to us will have a front-row seat as we try to implement what we have promised.

> " Charlotte Valeur, the former chair of the Institute of Directors, talks openly about how she makes her own values visible:
>
> Consciously living by your values can form an important guide in your life. It will help you make the right decisions easier and steer you away from areas that will undermine your integrity. But how do you do that in practice? I believe we have three levels of leadership: leading self, leading a team collaboratively and leading beyond yourself – creating an environment that makes other people successful.
>
> To become a leader at the third level, it is imperative that you lead with strong core values. To do so you need to consciously know what your own core values are. Think about the key three to five value words that relate to how you have lived, how you live now and how you intend to live going forward. One way to do that is to google 'ethical values' and look over the list to see which ones stand out for you. This is the first social values contract that you write with yourself. This is you leading yourself by defining your core values. You can then let friends and family know, as well as team members. By declaring them you create a sort of social contract – an agreement about the kind of person you want to be.
>
> The final step is to publicly announce your core values. This is a step many people find scary. You can do this by having your values as the headline on your social media, such as LinkedIn or Twitter. This is the step where you lead beyond yourself. By openly declaring your own specific values you also make yourself vulnerable and accountable. You give people the ability to point out if you behave in a way that is not according to your values. This, in turn, will be a great opportunity to grow with your values on an ongoing basis. It makes it more likely that you live and behave in a way that keeps your integrity in place. For me, integrity is what you have when you live by your values and what is yours to lose if you don't.

In the example above, Charlotte Valeur says, 'By openly declaring your own specific values you also make yourself vulnerable and accountable.' For that reason, we think it is important to enrol your closest colleagues in the process of deciding what public promises you should make as a leader. You need their buy-in and support, and you may also need their help.

In Chapter 4, we noted the importance of developing a healthy ego. Imperfect leaders lead with nuance when making public declarations or promises. They know that what they say, if not worded carefully, could be viewed as an egotistical over-promise from leaders who are so sure of themselves and their own competency that they make promises which sound egotistical or set themselves up to fail. It is therefore important that we display humility when making public promises.

 Steve

For twelve years, I made an annual speech to a large conference of school leaders in the UK. Over the course of those years, I increasingly talked about my own personal challenges as a leader and about the kind of leadership behaviours that I believed were most important. Having read my speeches, one of the education minister's special advisers said to me, 'You are trying to model in your speeches the leadership you want to see in schools.' He was exactly right on that one, but I was also modelling the kind of behaviours that I wanted to see in my own leadership. I talked about the importance of integrity, authenticity and leading with moral purpose. Since I knew that all of my colleagues at the National College, or later at the Education Development Trust, would be either reading or watching the speech, I recognised that I would have to continue to demonstrate authenticity in my leadership – or be accused of the worst kind of hypocrisy. Speaking publicly about authentic leadership helped to keep me focused on being an authentic leader. It reinforced my behaviours in a good way.

What are good promises?

Good public promises are aligned to the vision and values of the school or organisation that we lead. We should be able to describe the reasoning behind each promise made. It must be clear how keeping that promise will help us as leaders, and those we lead, to thrive. For public promises to be effective, people have to understand why they matter. Good public promises are active, explicit and communicated in a way that reinforces the vision of the school or organisation, as well as your own core values. Finally, a promise made in public should remain public throughout the life of the commitment – a good promise is visible.

 ## Marie-Claire

I once came across a head teacher who had been on the receiving end of lots of complaints from teachers about poor behaviour in lessons. The head teacher responded by inviting a behaviour specialist to lead a series of staff training sessions, and then at the end of the training said, 'If any of you continue to find the behaviour of students in your lessons difficult to manage, I will be more than happy to personally teach your class for you so that you can observe good behaviour management in practice.'

This public promise led to a number of teachers taking him up on his offer. The head teacher found it much harder than he anticipated. He struggled to demonstrate the theory of good behaviour management in practice, and as a result lost some credibility with his staff team. The intention behind the promise was honourable – a supportive opportunity to see good practice – but the precise offer of help was not well thought-through and exposed the leader. A better promise would have been to enable an opportunity for every teacher who requested it the chance to observe other lessons or visit other schools where there were demonstrable strengths in behaviour management.

Prompts for personal reflection

▪ To what extent have you defined your core values as a leader, and when and do you use them to guide you in making public promises?

▪ Before making a public promise, think about exactly what you are promising – have you got the time, power, focus and ability to keep that promise? How will you keep yourself on track? Who will help to keep you focused? How will you check up on how well you are doing?

▪ Have you ever made a public promise or seen a colleague do so? What was the impact? What could you learn from this in your own leadership?

Imperfect leaders elicit public promises from others

In this chapter so far, we have focused primarily on making public promises about our own leadership behaviours and approaches. But it is worth considering how the concept of making public promises can be applied on a wider scale.

Imperfect leaders that engender well-made, reliable promises within their school or organisation create a sense of community and shared purpose. In this way, we can establish collective commitment and foster a mutual sense of obligation to keep the promises we make to one another. These sorts of shared promises can help to stoke the passions of our colleagues and even our students. People promise to do things because they know how it supports the overall vision and priorities of the school or organisation; they see that they have a part to play and that creates a momentum for change.

Margaret Wheatley (2002, p. 55) puts it like this: 'There is no power for change greater than a community discovering what it cares about.' When we identify what really matters to the people we lead, we discover that it is easy to cultivate collective commitment to achieve that ambition together. However, imperfect leaders know that they must weave and manage these webs of promises with great care, encouraging iterative conversation to make sure commitments are understood and fulfilled reliably.

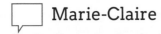 Marie-Claire

In 2010, the Department for Education in England announced that they planned to designate a number of national teaching schools. This was a policy initiative designed to empower high-performing schools to create and lead partnerships of schools with a remit to train new teachers and leaders, lead professional development, engage in research and evidence-based practice, and provide support to schools that were struggling and needed help to improve. The aim was that these alliances would become self-sustaining and self-improving, as described by David Hargreaves (2010, 2012), and that they would lead to improved outcomes for children and young people.

In 2013, I found myself leading a teaching school and a teaching school alliance in Lincolnshire, called KYRA. As we began our work together, it was very clear to me that if this voluntary partnership of schools was going to do meaningful work, then we needed to have a shared ambition and collective ownership of the alliance. Although we had a mandate from the Department for Education to do this work, it was always going to be more powerful to have a mandate from one another. To this end, we invited international consultant and facilitator Maggie Farrar to work with us as a group of school leaders to articulate what we wanted to achieve together, what our shared vision was for the alliance and, critically, what our commitment was to each other – our public promises.

These promises have become known as the KYRA DNA and they have driven our behaviours as an alliance during the last eight years:

- **Ambitious for children.** Always setting the bar high, even if it makes us feel uncomfortable, because by working together anything is possible.

- **A learning community.** Constantly understanding our needs and identifying best practice and research to generate a professional learning community. We are not afraid of asking for help, and nor are we reserved in offering support and expertise wherever we can.

- **Builders of social capital.** Starting with the premise 'What can we give?' rather than 'What can we get?' generates a rich community of mutual support and professional generosity.

- **Quality and impact.** Holding ourselves to account with clear aims and targets that clearly link to children's outcomes. As contributors, we will be open to the scrutiny of others, knowing that accountability and review is key to the continued success of any learning community.

- **Celebrating diversity.** Respecting the diversity of schools and members across our alliance. Seeing this as a strength whilst ensuring no one is excluded or left behind.

- **Moral purpose.** Committed to the success of children and adults in all of our schools. Our opportunity is to achieve something truly transformational that translates into a better education system for all. We celebrate the successes of our partners as we would our own.

As a group of school leaders, we have revisited these promises annually to reflect on how well we are doing. We share these reflections and evaluations with one another publicly so that we can learn and improve our community of practice. This has included examining the impact we have had on student outcomes in all our schools and how well we have collectively supported one another to improve our schools as judged by Ofsted, as well as whether we have got the right balance of participation through genuine giving and receiving within the partnership.

It is worth noting that in 2020 the Department for Education announced the end of the teaching school alliance initiative. However, KYRA has become self-sustaining and is carrying on without the support of the department. From my perspective, this is because of the promises our school leaders have made to one another in the alliance – they are far deeper and more meaningful than any Department for Education top-down mandate to collaborate. KYRA has continued to thrive and grow as a partnership of schools, with over 70 schools and school leaders committing to the KYRA DNA.

A promise made in public is a powerful driver and motivator. It can be the glue that holds communities together as they discover what matters to them.

Prompts for personal reflection

- What barriers exist to limit a sense of collective responsibility in your network?

- How might modelling imperfect leadership, including public promising, help?

Summary

Making a public promise can be a powerful aspect of an imperfect leader's approach:

- It can help us to remain focused on the things that matter the most.

- It can help us to stay true to the behaviours that we know we ought to be demonstrating.

- It can help to build a sense of collective responsibility.

Some guidelines for making public promises:

- Make them rarely and thoughtfully.

- Make them about your own behaviour and actions.

- When there is something that is really important for you to do as a leader, make a public promise as a way to avoid getting sidetracked.

- Make them as a way of building trust with your colleagues and positively influencing the culture in the organisation.

- Make them with others as a way of developing collective responsibility and ensuring commitment across the group.

- Ensure that they are intentionally and very publicly underpinned by values.

 ## Exercises to try

- Promise-keeping is linked inextricably to trust. Consider asking your colleagues whether leaders in your school or organisation always keep their promises. Reflect on the feedback you get. Make a list of the steps you could take to strengthen promise-keeping in your school or organisation.

- How good are you at keeping the promises you make? Do you ever find that you get to a Friday afternoon and remember that you haven't done that thing you promised yourself you would do this week? Try talking to a colleague about what you want to achieve and asking them to check in on you to see if you have done it.

Chapter 6
Being a Restless Learner

Learning is the only thing the mind never exhausts, never fears, and never regrets. It is one thing that will never fail us.

Anon.

If we have an imperfect leadership mindset then we understand that we are never the finished product. We love to explore new ideas; we are open to learning from our experiences; we have an insatiable desire to build knowledge and understanding about ourselves and about the people and organisations we lead. We are restless learners and we are persistently curious. Being a restless learner is about knowing that there is always more – more to learn about ourselves as people and leaders and more to learn about the world around us. Being a restless learner means we are open to being challenged, ready to change our minds and curious about how others see the world.

The role of the school leader as a factor in successful schools has been established through decades of school effectiveness research. We know that the quality of school leadership can make a very significant difference to the performance of teachers and, subsequently, outcomes for students (Sammons et al., 1995). Being a restless learner is about being driven to ensure that our impact is increasingly positive for the teachers we lead and the students for whom we are responsible.

A recent study from the United States suggests that the impact of good school leadership is even more important than previously thought. It concludes that there is a 'need for renewed attention to strategies for cultivating, selecting, preparing, and supporting a high-quality principal workforce', and adds that 'it is difficult to envision an investment in K–12 education with a higher ceiling on its potential return than improving school leadership' (Grissom et al., 2021, pp. xvii, xiv).

This is why imperfect leaders are restless learners. We know that the quality of our leadership can make a significant difference to the success of our students and colleagues, and that we therefore need to be the best leader we can be. If we mess up – and we sometimes do – we learn from our mistakes and try to do it better next time. We worry about having got it wrong today (sometimes we worry too much), but we are even more concerned about getting it right tomorrow.

Some leaders seem to think that learning to be a leader is like getting taller; eventually you get as tall as you are ever going to be and then you stop growing. In the same way, some leaders think that once you have reached a certain stage in your career as a leader, you then stop needing to learn anything else. You have arrived. You know it all. We have even seen, on occasion, some very experienced leaders react against being invited to participate in leadership development programmes – as if the invitation was some kind of insult and implied an element of inadequacy.

In contrast, restless learners have a deep curiosity about leadership and about how they can lead better – they are always open to learning. They know that they can learn from leaders who are further along the journey than they are, as well as from new leaders with fresh eyes and new insights. Imperfect leaders know that believing they have nothing to learn as a leader is a bad place to be. They acknowledge that they don't know everything, that they are going to make mistakes, and even fail sometimes, and they use this knowledge to propel them as learners.

Developing openness to learn

The good news is that developing openness to learning is something that leaders can practise and improve upon. Here are some approaches that we have found helpful in learning how to be a restless learner.

Cultivate self-compassion

Self-compassion is particularly important when we want to reflect and learn from failure or from mistakes. When we want to explore why something hasn't gone according to plan or why something didn't work, then we need to begin by accepting the failure or the mistake and then practise being compassionate with ourselves as we set out to explore and examine what happened. Rather than being defensive, angry or hiding away, we must take our shortcomings for what they are – an opportunity for growth – and be kind to ourselves as we explore them. It is helpful to think of self-compassion as extending understanding and encouragement to ourselves when we feel inadequate, when we have failed or when we are in the midst of suffering.

A practical way to do this is to imagine that you are sitting in a coffee shop with a close friend and they are telling you what happened in an authentic way – they explain what they were trying to do, what they had hoped would happen, as well as the mistakes they made along the way. What tone would you take in response? What questions would you ask them? How would you help them to open up? Sometimes we need to adopt a compassionate tone with ourselves too.

Developing a healthy open-to-learning mindset means that we can stay receptive to what new knowledge we can gain and what each experience has to teach us.

 ## Marie-Claire

The way I practise self-compassion is by reminding myself that I made the best decision I could given the available information and resources I had at the time.

Give yourself time to reflect

Deep reflection on our own practice is the very essence of great learning and good leadership. Reflecting on how we approach particular situations, being very mindful of what we are doing in the moment, and then reflecting later on about what went well and what we could have done differently, is how we learn to lead. Reflection is about stepping back to consider what we have learned so that we can be better in the future – and it is a great habit to cultivate.

One practical way to do this is to routinely allocate an hour a week in your schedule for reflection. We recognise that this can be hard to do with the busyness of the school environment, but it can be really powerful for leaders when they prioritise their own self-development and improvement. When you take time to reflect, don't shy away from asking yourself tough questions – replay conversations and situations in your mind and consider whether you had the impact you wanted. Rehearse and plan future conversations and interactions – how can you be a better leader in those moments? Without meaningful reflection we tend to be reactive in our leadership and follow our instincts. By using deep reflection we can be more intentional and more mindful in our leadership, and avoid mistakes, bad reactions and leading by instinct.

 ## Marie-Claire

Why not use the journey to and from school to reflect? Ask questions of yourself like: when was I at my best today, and why? What made me curious today, and why? If I was to repeat today, what would I have done/said differently, and why? What motivated me to say/do X, Y or Z? Keep examining yourself.

Become a better version of yourself

We all make mistakes, and it is important that we give ourselves permission to do so. But some leaders are able to be at their best more often because they reflect on their mistakes and then they apply what they are learning in a more effective way. Reducing variation within our own leadership is a great skill. Outstanding leaders aren't necessarily better leaders than the rest of us; they just operate at their best more often.

Steve

When I was a director of education in Knowsley, we had too few students for the number of secondary schools in the locality and many of the school buildings were run-down and no longer adequate. We managed to procure some significant funding from the government to rebuild all the secondary schools in the area. This was great news, but the student numbers meant that we brought forward proposals to close down all the existing schools and open fewer new ones.

When people are faced with change – even if it may well be in their long-term best interests – there will always be those who will resist it. Many parents and staff wanted to hold on to things as they were, for understandable reasons. As part of the consultation process, I decided that I would lead all the public meetings. I expected a bumpy ride, but it was even worse than I expected. At the first public meeting, I found the anger, the upset and the personal attacks extremely hard to deal with. At the end of the meeting, after everyone had left, I burst into tears. Then I thought to myself: I have another twelve of these public meetings to do. I cannot spend much of the next three months in tears!

I reflected upon what I had found so difficult and how I might prevent some of those very difficult moments from happening again. Gradually, I honed my expertise at handling these situations – reviewing my mistakes and trying out different ways of managing the meetings. Each time I tried to be better than the last time, and eventually I became quite confident about leading those public meetings.

Marie-Claire

I know one leader who started her journaling habit by writing a sentence a day beginning with the words: 'Today I was at my best when …' She grew this habit to include a weekly reflection starting with: 'If I could do one thing this week again, differently or better, what would I do and why?'

Deep reflection can be powerful, but it really only has an impact when it influences subsequent action. We have found that keeping a journal and making notes about what we are learning and what we are curious about is a useful way to document the agreements we make with ourselves about what we are going to try to do next as a leader and what we want to learn more about. We mentioned this earlier in Chapter 4 in relation to developing a healthy ego. Even the brilliant Leonardo da Vinci needed to write things down in a notebook so he could remember what he needed to do next and what he was curious about. In one extract from his notebooks, Toby Lester notes the repetition of the phrase *dimmi*, which means 'tell me'. Leonardo writes: 'Tell me, ... tell me whether, ... tell me how things are, ... tell me if there was ever ...' Lester (2012, p. 94) describes these as 'the tics of an increasingly hungry mind'; we would describe him as a restless and curious learner.

 ## Prompt for personal reflection

- Sometimes we see other leaders and we want to copy them. There is nothing wrong with that. We have tried to follow in the footsteps of leaders we have admired and have tried to learn from them. But, in the end, leaders have to learn to walk in their own shoes. Rather than copy others, imperfect leaders try to improve on their own previous best. Can you think of a particular moment or stretch of time in your leadership experience when you have been at your best? With these examples in mind, describe the kind of leader you want to become more like and write it down. What did you do well and what do you want to continue to do well?

Adopt a growth mindset

Over thirty years ago, Professor Carol Dweck coined the phrases 'growth mindset' and 'fixed mindset' to describe the underlying beliefs that learners have about themselves. A growth mindset means believing that skills and abilities are not set in stone. A fixed mindset is the belief that you are who you are and that change and growth as a learner isn't possible. Being a restless learner is about believing that growth and learning is possible.

When we make mistakes, we can end up thinking that we have failed as a leader and attribute the failure to our ability or our core identity – who we think we are. In fact, we know some leaders who, in the face of a mistake or failure, default to the position that they haven't got what it takes, that they aren't good enough, or that they cannot work any harder or do it any better. A healthier position is to adopt the belief that we might be able to be more successful if we reflect and then use the learning to try an alternative approach, to do something new or to take a different direction. In order to be open to learn, it is helpful to think about our mistakes as a failure in strategy, approach or execution, not a failure in identity or ability.

 ## Marie-Claire

As a young head teacher, I often sought advice from my dad (I still do!). He was a successful secondary principal in Northern Ireland and inspires me in many ways, both as a person and as a leader. In my first year of headship there were times when I felt like things were really getting on top of me. In the evenings and at weekends I would be consumed with thinking about work and unable to shake the feeling of frustration and failure. In some ways, I was reflecting too much and giving myself a hard time about the things I was finding difficult and the mistakes I felt I was making.

My dad had a phrase – he said, 'Wear it outside of yourself.' What he meant was treat work, with all its pressures, mistakes and challenges, like a coat that you put on when you go to work and take off when you get home. This concept has been profoundly helpful to me in learning that the criticism and pressure I sometimes feel in a work context does not define me as a person. I can stop overthinking, I don't have to wear the coat all the time – I can switch off. But, equally, there are times (with the coat on) when I need to reflect deeply and think about my leadership, my mistakes and what I am learning. Becoming disciplined with my time, by scheduling time to reflect and think, has helped me to manage this more successfully.

Avoiding the plateau

Earlier in this chapter, Steve described how he used self-reflection to improve his practice in leading and managing public meetings. In this particular example there was a sense of urgency – he had public meetings every week, he wanted to lead the meetings better and he wanted a way to stop himself crying afterwards! The experience was a new one for Steve as a leader: the feedback on his performance was instant and the need to adjust his approach and master the task at hand was pressing.

Similarly, teachers get instant feedback in the classroom, particularly when the lesson goes wrong. This is especially true for teachers who are in the very early stages of their career. They usually receive regular feedback from mentors following observations and peer teaching, but they also get very direct and immediate responses from the students themselves. Students tend to let teachers know when lessons aren't going well; they can look bored or misbehave. If they are going to make a success of teaching, inexperienced teachers notice this feedback, adjust their practice and try to improve. In addition, it is worth noting that teachers in their first two years of teaching are always doing things for the first time. As a result, they need to plan each lesson very deliberately; they cannot rely on previous experience or learned habits. The experience of teaching is new, the feedback is more frequent than at any other point in their career and, therefore, the learning curve is steeper.

Becky Allen (2019, p. 112) explains that:

> Thankfully, through trial and error, most new teachers can acquire the initial toolkit of classroom routines that are needed to overcome the chaos of those early days. Many have drawn analogies between the process a new teacher goes through and Ericsson's deliberate practice cycle (Ericsson et al., 1993), for they must:
>
> - 01 Try out a new and specific technique
> - 02 Receive feedback on whether or not it worked
> - 03 Adjust their practice in light of the feedback.

However, after the first two years or so, teachers develop habits that reduce the negative feedback. Their teaching becomes more instinctive and more habitual. This is an entirely good thing. We don't think many people would cope if teaching was as stressful and as hard work as it is in their first year or two. As they become expert teachers, they can cut some corners and build on what they have done before. But there is a big downside to this: they become much less adept at learning new skills. As teachers develop a repertoire of reasonably effective teaching techniques, the feedback from students is less evident, as fewer things go badly wrong. At the same time, their practice becomes consolidated in long-term memory and in doing so becomes automated and therefore insensitive to any feedback they do receive. The habits of the classroom are needed to make teaching fluent, but they also actively stop teachers from adapting their practice to improve.

The whole purpose of schools is learning, and yet it is interesting that in some cases teachers seem to stop learning and developing. It is the role of school leaders to help to create the climate that enables teachers to want to continue to learn and to be supported in doing so. This is why focused and effective professional development, peer-to-peer review, collaboration and coaching are so important.

Just as teachers can find themselves plateauing in their learning and development, once they have developed instinctive ways of teaching, the same can be said for leadership. When we start in a leadership role, especially if it is in a new school, we often find ourselves having to make decisions about things we have never considered before. It can be quite stressful, as we struggle to make sense of our new context and understand the people with whom we are working. But, after a while, some of those things become less taxing, as we familiarise ourselves with the individuals and the issues. Of course, there will always be new challenges (we are writing this during a pandemic), but some of the basic knowledge and understanding necessary will, hopefully, have been achieved.

So, the challenge after a few years is to avoid our leadership plateauing. Like teachers, leaders can form habits and develop ways of behaving that have served them well in the past and have become instinctive. This can make it harder for leaders to change in the future, when there may be fewer crises and fewer completely new issues to address. Complacency can slowly creep up on us. We think that what we are doing and how we are leading is fine. We are still working hard. We are still putting in the hours. We are still dealing with loads of challenges. We are still reviewing the data, holding meetings and writing reports. But, actually, we may have lost our drive and our absolute determination to improve things. We may have stopped asking ourselves the really hard questions. We may not be actively seeking out, with as much enthusiasm as we used to, what is not going as well as it might and confronting it. We may not be looking for external challenge as much as we did previously. And the most worrying thing about complacency is that we may not realise we have got it.

 ## Steve

I remember many years ago being involved in a review of a primary school. We found that each class did art on a Wednesday afternoon, which at the time stretched the scarce resources in the school. So, we asked why they all did art on a Wednesday and were told that it was because the caretaker liked to organise the cleaning on the Wednesday. We therefore went to see the caretaker and challenged him on it. He replied that he didn't mind what day of the week the teachers taught art. We responded by saying that the teachers had told us that it had to be on a Wednesday because of him. To which he replied, 'Oh, that must have been the previous caretaker – he retired a few years ago.' It is fascinating that in this case the school's curriculum was being driven by the caretaker who had retired some years previously! The school was just continuing to do what it had always done without questioning why. This may be an extreme example, but how many of the routines in our schools are there not for any good reason but just because they have always been done that way? Have we become so close to our own institution that we no longer ask the 'why' questions?

Grown-up and restless leadership

Imperfect leaders are restless learners and continue to ask the why questions. We want to combine the wisdom of the experienced leader with the enthusiasm of the novice leader. Consider Figure 6.1. Even relatively young leaders can find themselves in the bottom left-hand quadrant – immature but already set in their ways, with fixed habits, a relatively closed mind and certain ways of doing things. In contrast, most of us start off in the bottom right-hand quadrant – full of enthusiasm, grand ideas and determination to make a big difference to children's lives, but we make lots of mistakes along the way as we gradually improve our leadership expertise. Unfortunately, some of us can end up in the top left-hand quadrant – we have developed the expertise to be a good leader, we have shown wisdom and sure-footedness and we have had some suc-cess, but we have stopped learning. External and internal pressures and the hard slog of implementation have begun to grind us down. We have become stagnant. We have lost our edge. Those with an imperfect leadership mindset aim to be in the top right-hand quadrant – they develop their leadership expertise and grow up as leaders, but they remain restless learners.

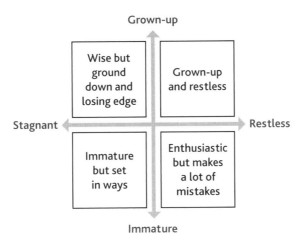

Figure 6.1. The restless learner matrix

In Chapter 1, we discussed how imperfect leaders are self-aware and how they contin-ually seek to become even more aware of the impact they have on others. In the case study that follows, Sir Peter Wanless shares a powerful personal example of how he systematically invited feedback in order to continually build a better awareness of him-self as a leader. There is a restlessness and an openness to grow and develop, which is an outlook and approach that Sir Peter has cultivated over many years. Imperfect leaders never stop trying to be more self-aware.

🔍 Case study

Sir Peter Wanless, CEO, National Society for the Prevention of Cruelty to Children

The National Society for the Prevention of Cruelty to Children (NSPCC) is a large UK-based charity. Before taking on the CEO role at NSPCC, I was CEO of a national funder of good causes, the Big Lottery, and before that I worked as a senior civil servant in the Department for Education in England.

After six years as CEO at NSPCC, I decided that it was time to open myself up more as a leader and to take action to ensure that I was avoiding complacency. I worked with an external coach, Jonathan Bowman-Perks, on an approach that came from Marshall Goldsmith and is called stakeholder-centred coaching. My aim was to adjust and improve my own leadership and, at the same time, to help build trust amongst my senior team by modelling the fact that I am a learner and that I welcome feedback. I also wanted to demonstrate and model that we are all imperfect leaders and that nobody is the finished article.

I carried out a 360° feedback process, seeking comments from my senior team, from others in the organisation and also from some external stakeholders. I used the feedback, in discussion with my coach, to identify two important areas for improvement in my leadership:

1. Have I got the balance right between pace and engagement? I was praised as an inclusive leader, but opinions differed on whether I was driving through change at sufficient pace. All agreed that variable pace was vital, but I was concerned that no one should experience what they might perceive as prevarication.

2. Building an inclusive team. I was clearly leading a team of high-performing individuals, but was I helping them to become an inclusive team and to be seen as such?

Each month I asked eight individuals from that cross-section of 360° feedback respondents to give me direct feedback on how I was doing on my two areas for improvement and to feed forward on what specifically I could do during the next month to improve further. I actively sought out this chosen few, and each month I would then circulate to them my simple reflections and priorities for the next four weeks.

After six months, I asked for specific feedback on these two development issues from all those who had completed the original 360° feedback for me, and I repeated this whole process again after eleven months.

My senior team also went through the same process to identify two key behaviours they would work on in a similarly open fashion.

As a team, this process required us to dedicate specific time to how we worked effectively with one another. We made clear progress in trusting each other and in being more inclusive as well as exposing specific tensions.

The whole organisation – not just the senior team – became more open to learning because many more people could see that I was actively trying to be a better leader myself, as opposed to issuing instructions and opportunities to others.

I was able to adjust my leadership behaviours. I was able to think more carefully about the kind of leadership that the organisation needed from me now, as opposed to the kind of leadership that they may have needed from me when I joined the NSPCC six years previously.

What I found hardest was having the discipline to ask people for feedback every month across a whole year. Yet those around me, without exception, were happy to be asked and genuinely honest in their contribution.

After six years, I was confident enough in myself as a leader to risk opening myself up in this way. I would probably have regarded this as too risky if I had done it in the first year or two of my time as CEO, when the immediate priorities of those who had appointed me were more obvious anyway.

Although challenging, it was also satisfying to see how I could still adapt my leadership and that my behaviours as a leader weren't so engrained that I couldn't adjust them.

Prompts for personal reflection

▪ What new experiences can you seek out for yourself that take you out of your comfort zone?

▪ How can you expose yourself to feedback to help you refine your leadership practice?

▪ Where can you open yourself up to external challenge?

▪ Can you take on a new personal challenge and look for a way to extend yourself and avoid the plateau?

 Marie-Claire

I am often inspired by the school leaders I meet and work with. But one head teacher in particular stands out as an example of a restless learner. James Siddle is the head teacher at a rural and coastal primary school called St Margaret's Church of England Primary School in Lincolnshire where there are only seventy pupils on roll. Despite being a teaching head teacher in a small school where capacity is limited, he has never stopped learning how to secure better outcomes for the pupils for whom he is responsible, and he has achieved impressive results over a number of years – in particular, for the disadvantaged pupils in his school. James is a great example of a restless learner – he has an insatiable desire to learn from research and evidence and then apply it to his practice as a teacher and a leader. He has been engaged in dozens of research projects with the Education Endowment Foundation, as well as with universities in England. It was this passion and commitment that led to him being seconded for two days a week to lead the KYRA Research School, and through that work to influence leaders and teachers right across the East Midlands with his passion for learning.

Imperfect leaders are curious about others

We have talked a lot in this chapter about being open to learning about yourself as a leader and remaining restless as a learner. Imperfect leaders are also restless in their desire to learn about others.

If we are to lead well and to continue learning, then we need to be open-minded. Imperfect leaders are slow to condemn or dismiss groups of people who genuinely seem to have a different view about an educational issue. They are curious rather than oppositional towards those who may see things differently. They ask, 'What's really going on here?' 'I wonder why these colleagues have such a different view from me?' 'What can I learn from them?' Of course, we need to have strong values and beliefs, and we need to be committed to evidence-based approaches, but we also need to be able to walk in the other person's shoes, to see things from their perspective, to combat intuitive bias. We need to have an approach which, as Viviane Robinson says, is more about 'truth-seeking' and less about 'truth-claiming' (Robinson et al., 2020).

This requires a level of comfort with ambiguity – the ability to see things from various points of view at the same time. It may sometimes lead to less certainty, which means that we may need to be honest about the fact that we don't know all the answers. As leaders, it shouldn't prevent us from making decisions; it just means that they are likely to be more thoughtful decisions.

As human beings we like to be part of a group, to feel that we belong, to hear people who have the same or similar views to the ones we hold, to mix with people who like the same things that we like. But polarisation and the forming of cliques or camps inevitably makes us less likely to consider all the available evidence rationally and objectively.

Seeing things from a narrow point of view is an easy mistake to make, and we need to work hard as leaders to resist it. The famous crime writer Agatha Christie said that the secret of solving a crime is keeping an open mind for as long as possible. The moment you make up your mind as to whom committed the murder, you only see the evidence that fits your thinking or, even worse, you begin to make the evidence fit your assumptions.

It is not always wrong to be in one faction against another – for example, we want to be in the opposite camp to racists and bigots. We don't want to give the impression that compromise is always the best way forward. But, overall, imperfect leaders understand that they don't know it all and that it is a dangerous place to be if they think they do. As imperfect leaders, we confront our own biases and prejudices by seeking out challenge and welcoming new ideas. We avoid groupthink. We ask ourselves, 'Why are these people thinking like that?' We have respectful dialogue with them.

Being an open-minded leader is not about being a weak leader. Far from it. This is not about wishy-washy or mediocre leadership. It is not all about compromise. It is about empathy, understanding and careful thought. It is about taking what is good and right from what appear to be opposing ideas and making something even better. In her 2020 podcast, in which she interviewed Barack Obama, Brené Brown said, 'People who can hold the discomfort of paradox are truly the most transformative leaders amongst us.' How can we, as imperfect leaders, hold the paradox in order to seek transformation?

Near where Steve lives in Manchester there is a place called Alderley Edge. As you approach, a fingerpost directs you one of two ways – along the flat and into the woods or the more challenging route 'to the edge'. This is a good image for the choices that face us as school leaders. Do we head for the woods and sit comfortably in one of the camps surrounded by people who agree with us, but failing to include or engage others who don't share our view and perhaps missing out on even better strategies that would improve our schools? Or do we choose to spend some time walking along the edge, even when it is uncomfortable, because we know that seeing more than one perspective is more likely to enable us to make better decisions.

Summary

6

Being a Restless
Learner

If we have an imperfect leadership mindset, we know that:

- We are never the finished product, so we are restless learners and remain open-minded and curious.

- We are eager to learn more about ourselves and how we lead, as well as how others see the world.

- We are comfortable with ambiguity and uncertainty, and we are open to changing our minds.

- We know that the quality of our leadership can make a big difference, so we learn from our mistakes and try to do better next time.

- We are kind to ourselves if we do make mistakes because we know that nobody is perfect and it gives us an opportunity to learn.

- We don't necessarily try to be exactly like another leader; instead, we try to be a better version of ourselves as a leader.

Exercises to try

- **Become more open to learning.** Are you able to articulate (to yourself) what you are learning about yourself as a leader at the moment? Use a journal to reflect on something you have done this week. What did you notice about yourself? Are there ways you would have liked to have done things differently, and why? Do you notice any patterns in how you lead, react or respond to things?

- **Create an open-to-learning culture.** Consider starting each one-to-one conversation with the question: 'What are you learning right now?' See if you can make talking about learning about leading part of the culture of your senior leadership team. Use books, blogs and YouTube videos to stimulate conversations about leadership. Remember to put yourself firmly in the camp of learner, too, and model curiosity.

- **Practise self-compassion.** Reflect on something that hasn't gone well or where you know you have made a mistake or failed. Write a letter to your former self as if from a good friend. What have you learned from this experience? What advice would you now give your former self? What might have led to a different outcome? What do you want to learn from this and apply next time?

- **Try changing places with one of your leadership team members for a day.** It will model that you are a learner and help you to have a greater understanding of their work.

- **Use 360° feedback in a focused and time-specific way to improve aspects of your leadership.** Consider engaging with a coach to help you clarify what you are learning and how you want to adjust or modify your leadership approach.

- **Invite peer review and use the process to seek feedback on your leadership and impact.** Peer review, when done well, can be a powerful process which supports leaders in continually learning, reflecting and leading change and improvement. Approaching peer review with an open-to-learn mindset models to the whole school community that you are still a learner and are restless to refine and improve your leadership and the school.

Chapter 7
Power and Love

Power without love is reckless and abusive, and love without power is sentimental and anemic.

Martin Luther King Jr

Imperfect leaders show power in their leadership, but they also show love.

Adam Kahane, an experienced adviser on solving complex national and international problems, argues that in order to address the toughest challenges we face in society, we must exercise both power and love. He defines power as 'the drive to achieve one's purpose, to get one's job done' and love as 'the drive to reconnect and make whole that which has become or appears fragmented' or 'the urge to unite with others' (Kahane, 2010, p. 2). He also argues that leaders need to be driven simultaneously by both power and love, echoing what was said by Martin Luther King Jr.

We believe that this idea of power and love also applies to the leadership of schools and organisations. The way that we see power and love in leadership is captured in Table 7.1 on page 132. The way that power and love work best is when they are exercised together. It is not power *or* love, it is power *and* love.

Table 7.1. Power and love in leadership

Power looks like	Love looks like
Driven leadership	Kind and compassionate leadership
Focused and determined	Inclusive and collaborative leadership
Indomitable	Builds relationships
Works with pace, urgency and agency	Takes people on the journey
Relentless in the pursuit of high expectations	Asks for help and participation
Strong accountability and high challenge	Empowers others
Assertive and confident	Humble
Focused on getting the job done	Empathetic

The importance of power in leadership

Power is about making a difference and getting things done. Drive and determination is essential if we want to improve our schools and make changes which have a positive and lasting impact. Schools need leaders who continually want to improve and change things for the better. Leaders who are strong, who challenge mediocre practice, who drive tirelessly towards improvement and who are determined to make a difference. Leaders who are pacey and authoritative and who understand that children only get one chance at school. Leaders who demonstrate power in their leadership are confident in holding people to account, and they are willing to hold courageous conversations which challenge poor practice or behaviour.

We often talk in education about leading with moral purpose, but moral purpose is not just about having good intentions, about being well-disposed towards children and young people or about wanting the best for them. We can often focus more on the moral part than the purpose part. Leading with moral purpose is about having the single-minded determination to change the things that will make a difference.

Leading with power means that we don't shy away from making tough decisions. Once we have made up our mind that a particular course of action is absolutely necessary, after taking advice and careful reflection, we are prepared to push things through in spite of opposition from some within the organisation. This is sometimes unavoidable when significant and radical change is needed – for example, during the first eighteen months in your role as CEO or head teacher if the organisation is in difficulty and in need of a fundamental overhaul. At times, this may feel very lonely and challenging, but this doesn't stop us driving forwards towards a better future for the organisation or school that we lead.

Without power in our leadership, our school is unlikely to improve. When resistance to change takes place, as is inevitable, we won't see it through. The school will drift and may even go backwards. We will end up being led by the school rather than leading it. Those who lead with power choose to do the hard stuff – not because they enjoy it but because they know it is the right thing to do in the interests of the children and young people. They choose to walk into the wind rather than settling for an easier time. Kahane (2010, p. 13) observes that 'without power nothing new grows'. Power is therefore an essential component of imperfect leadership, of growth and improvement. As Claire Amos says in her case study on page 136, we have to help our colleagues to 'brave the learning pit'.

The dangers of power without love in leadership

Leading with power can become unhealthy if it is not combined with love. For example, a healthy version of leading with power means that leaders have a belief that they have a 'power to' achieve things together with their colleagues. If this slips into a 'power over' mindset, leaders can become controlling or even oppressive. Imperfect leaders lead with a 'power to' mindset – they know they have the power to make a difference and they do this by combining power with love.

Steve

I remember when I worked for a local authority many years ago and was called to the director of education's office for a breakfast meeting. It was a big thing to be asked to attend a meeting with the director; I was nervous but at least I was looking forward to my breakfast. When I arrived at his office there was a long table with him at the head, his senior officials sitting along each side and a chair for me at the end. It was at this moment that I realised that it was indeed a breakfast meeting, but the director of education was the only one allowed to have a breakfast! The rest of us sat there, watching him eat, and duly received our instructions on what needed to be done in the local authority. It was an uncomfortable and challenging experience, and then I left the room – still hungry! The director was demonstrating to everyone that he was the important, powerful person and we were less important. He was demonstrating his 'power over' us. This man was a great strategist, and over the years I came to appreciate his strengths far more, but at the time I didn't want to follow him or emulate him. Power without love in leadership can alienate.

Leaders who overly rely on power, rather than a combination of power and love, tend to create a culture that depends on challenge and accountability to motivate their teams. This can lead to some short-term success. However, fear and accountability are not enough to motivate people in the long term. If we lead with power, and not with power and love, we will just end up with exhausted and demotivated staff who feel done to and done in.

For example, people with chronic heart disease may well have been told by their health-care professionals that their life chances are in jeopardy if they don't change their lifestyle. Many people who have heard this sort of challenge from a GP or a nurse do make changes to their diet and try to exercise more. But more often than not these changes only last a short period of time. It is much harder to change behaviour in the long term. People who do make sustained changes often cite the importance of the love and support of their family and friends as they make significant lifestyle changes. It is the combination of the challenge and concerns raised by the medics (power) and the sense of support and care from others (love) that makes the difference.

Leading with power can also be understood as pace-setting leadership. Daniel Goleman (2000) argues that although pace-setting is an important leadership style and is sometimes just what is needed, it won't provide lasting improvements unless you also adopt other leadership styles as well. As leaders, if our only style is pace-setting, we may find that we have stepped out on our own and nobody is following – instead, they are criticising us from the sidelines.

 Steve

In 2007, on the INSEAD Advanced Management programme, we spent half a day analysing former UK Prime Minister Margaret Thatcher's leadership. She was a remarkable leader; extremely knowledgeable, always on top of her brief, confident and determined. She took on the status quo and changed it. She did not shy away from courageous conversations. She demonstrated great power in her leadership. Those who worked for her and with her – in her cabinet and in her private office – admired and respected her. But she failed to demonstrate much love in her leadership. She was divisive rather than inclusive in style. She could bully people and talk down to them. People like the Chancellor Geoffrey Howe were demeaned by her. Whilst the leader is powerful and the organisation is successful, he or she will continue to command respect, but if that success starts to wither then loyalty from colleagues isn't always forthcoming. Howe eventually resigned and made a withering (and quite out-of-character) speech against her in the House of Commons and many of her cabinet turned against her when she needed them most. Reciprocity works both ways. Those who show love (as well as power) in their leadership are more likely to receive loyalty and support in return.

The dangers of love without power in leadership

Some leaders can focus so much on the love side of leadership that not much gets done; so much time is spent on consultation and collaboration that decisions are slow and lack agility. There is a failure to hold people to account, those who are not pulling their weight aren't challenged, problems are not addressed and challenging conversations rarely take place. The result is complacency and cosiness. People describe the leader as a nice person, but they get frustrated because nothing improves.

But love without power in leadership can also be more subtle than that. Leaders who put love strongly before power can tend to do things themselves – even when it isn't their job – rather than asking others to do them because they want to be kind. If this becomes a pattern, colleagues will increasingly take the more difficult and challenging tasks to the leader rather than do them themselves. The result is burnout for the leader and a reduction in the capacity of the organisation to improve itself. Tracey Ezard explains this well in her book, *Ferocious Warmth: School Leaders Who Inspire and Transform* (2021).

In the following case study, Claire Amos recounts how, in her first principalship, she set out to be a 'warm and demanding change leader'. She developed a shared approach based on common values and mission, but she challenged her staff and kept her expectations very high: 'whilst we weren't willing to remove the pressure, we were willing to acknowledge that they were feeling challenged. Our messaging to staff was to keep talking to us! Look after your health and well-being.'

 ## Case study

Claire Amos, tumuaki/principal, Albany Senior High School, Auckland, New Zealand

Albany Senior High School (ASHS) is a senior only (Years 11–13) modern learning environment in New Zealand. It opened its doors to students in 2009 and has now grown to a roll of over 850. From its inception, ASHS was defined by its innovative approaches, with a three-pronged curriculum that spans specialist subjects, tutorials and a dedicated day of cross-curricular project-based learning every Wednesday. Whilst ASHS has experienced the normal challenges of any school doing things differently, it continues to be a school that is recognised for its innovation. It has established a solid reputation and has a settled and experienced team of teachers.

I came into the school in the middle of the academic year in 2018 as a first-time principal. I have been in education for over twenty years and came to this role with an established reputation as a change leader, particularly in the educational technology and educational futures space. I joined ASHS knowing that I loved the curriculum design and the way that the time allocations clearly signalled the value of each element. I knew that I loved the timetable, made up of 300 blocks a day with time committed to subjects, projects and academic coaching. What I did not know was how well each element (in their current form) was meeting the needs of each and every learner. And, as in every school, there is often a disconnect between our espoused theory and our theory in action.

Whilst I could have sent out a survey or Google Form to gather perceptions, I knew nothing could beat actually observing students and teachers in their environment.

Observing teachers in their habitat

Over my first term as principal, I prioritised spending my time in the classrooms, documenting everything I was seeing and hearing. And in the spirit of being open and transparent, I thought it was only fair that I shared with our teachers the lens through which I was to observe the teaching and learning taking place. When I judged if learning was powerful, I often asked myself three questions: is learning visible? Is learning deep? Is learning inclusive?

Identifying the problem – are we walking the walk?

In observing teachers and students, I recognised that not walking the walk was a common issue in many (if not all) schools. We had an incredible curriculum and timetable underpinned by fabulous mantras such as, 'It's not if you're bright, it's how you're bright!', 'No one slips through the cracks' and 'We will always be a new school!' And for the most part we had a team that really believed in these ideas. They could talk the talk, but over time it seemed that we were failing to walk the walk. For a myriad of reasons, practices had slipped into various degrees of auto-pilot. This raised further questions for myself and for the leadership team: how effectively are our teachers living out our vision and/or mantra? Do they actually know what it looks like in practice? How can we coach and co-design how to walk the walk?

Sharing ownership and co-designing the solution

For me, leading change has always been about sharing the ownership of the challenges, the change needed and co-designing a solution to any issues we identify. The points of reference were as follows: what do we value? What are the beliefs about learning which underpin a particular practice, and are they reasonable beliefs based on current research on how we learn? How does our current practice help us to achieve what we value? How will a suggested different practice improve our ability to achieve what we value and believe?

In order to co-design solutions, we used the work of Dr Julia Atkin and her paper 'From values to beliefs about learning to principles and practice' (1996).

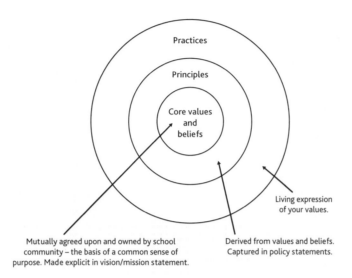

The relationship between core values and beliefs and practices (Atkin, 1996, p. 4)

Being prepared for staff feeling challenged and braving the learning pit

Once we had supported teachers to articulate and understand our school values and what our beliefs meant in terms of principles and, in turn, practices, making the changes meant a lot of complex work and led to a school-wide focus on universal design for learning and responsive assessment practices.

This, of course, led to staff feeling challenged, and whilst we weren't willing to remove the pressure, we were willing to acknowledge that they were feeling challenged. Our messaging to staff was to keep talking to us. Look after your health and well-being. You have control of your day after 3.10pm. Ensure you build in time to switch off. Understanding change is actually not that hard. Change is uncomfortable. Support one another. Share your tips and strategies with one another. Remain curious about why your students are disengaged (if they are).

Remember to embrace and celebrate your teacher agency. You can do whatever you need to make learning more manageable, creative and engaging.

We also acknowledged and normalised the idea of what James Nottingham (2017) calls getting into 'the learning pit'. We encouraged our teachers to get into the pit and also see if they could help others out. We owned the challenge of finding the right mix of being warm and demanding. I owned the fact that we were always finding the balance of positive pressure and looking after staff well-being, and that we would never apologise for demanding the very best for our young people. At all times, clearly communicating shared moral purpose was key.

Being a warm and demanding change leader and leading to the North-East

In New Zealand we have a seminal text, *Teaching to the North-East: Relationship-Based Learning in Practice* (Bishop, 2019), which is informed by the belief that in order to achieve the best outcomes for learners, we need high relationships and high teaching skills. In my journey as a new principal, I often thought about what it might look like if we are to lead to the North-East and how this might support leading change as a warm and demanding leader. This meant creating a family-like context for learning and a well-managed learning environment. It meant leaders holding and voicing high expectations for all their teachers and colleagues; giving teachers critical feedback so they know where they are at in their teaching, what is working well and where they need to go next; and creating opportunities for co-designing how initiatives will be rolled out.

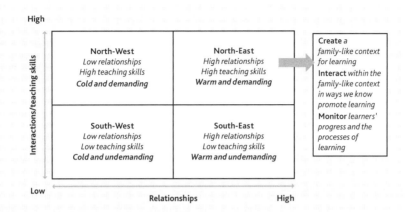

Teaching to the North-East (originally Bishop, 2019; later adapted by Abraham, 2020)

2021 marked my third anniversary as principal at ASHS and it is heartening to reflect on how we have come together in closing the gap between our espoused practice and practice in theory. Now, for me, being a warm demander means that I try to be my normal authentic self. Regularly and clearly articulating what is expected of all staff. Reminding people, 'We don't talk about students like that here …' Noticing and celebrating great practice. Owning, acknowledging and apologising for mistakes. But, most importantly, never apologising for demanding the very best for our young people.

The importance of love in leadership

Love in leadership is about connecting with people, bringing people together and uniting people with purpose. Imperfect leaders know that many of their colleagues lead complicated lives, and that what they need most from their leaders is to be understood, to feel valued and to be able to make a meaningful contribution at work. Our colleagues need to know that we see them, that we value their work, that their voice is listened to and that they are all playing an important part in the success of the organisation.

In 2017, the Department for Education in England commissioned a study to examine how teachers felt about their workload, and in particular how that correlated to their desire to stay in their school or leave their school (or indeed the profession) (Sims, 2017). The feedback suggested that teachers with the same or similar workloads differ in their assessment of whether that work is manageable and whether or not they want to move school.

Despite similar levels of workload, in the schools where teachers reported high satisfaction rates and a low desire to leave, the difference was that they felt their leaders valued them and that their work was important and fulfilling: 'Looking at the school working conditions, Leadership/Management emerges as having by far the strongest association with both job satisfaction and desire to move school … highlighting the critical importance of school leadership for teacher retention' (Sims, 2017, pp. 19–20).

Imperfect leaders know that love in leadership means valuing people and connecting them to a meaningful purpose. Without the love, people are more likely to be unhappy and dissatisfied at work.

Some might think leading with love sounds fluffy or superfluous, an added extra, and that what we really need is powerful leaders, perhaps with a bit of emotional intelligence on the side. We believe that leading with love can be transformative, if it is combined with power. Love gives people dignity, it gives them meaning and it unites them with their purpose. Leading with love is not weak; it is the context which opens up possibilities and reveals potential.

 Marie-Claire

Several years ago, I had a teacher working for me who wasn't doing a very good job in his teaching role. What was clear, though, was that the children adored him – he was a talented singer and performer and, in my opinion, he would have made a wonderful children's TV presenter! But he wasn't a great teacher. He struggled to manage his pupils' learning, he couldn't sequence his lessons or pitch the work well, and his ability to respond in the moment to pupils in terms of effective feedback was weak. After a term of intensive support, we decided that we needed to put him on a support plan and follow the school's capability policy. The pupils just weren't making the necessary progress.

Despite some periods when he was absent, we continued to work our way through the process of providing the right levels of support and challenge. I felt able simultaneously to see the potential that this individual had – potential to work with children and young people in a different context, whilst at the same time find the strength to say that he wasn't improving as a teacher and that we would need to take action to secure better teaching for the pupils in the school.

It took time, but in the end, we were able to move him on with full union engagement. At the end of the process, in our last meeting, he welled up and said that he knew we had done all we could, and that, despite the difficult process, he felt he had been seen and understood, and that he was now going to pursue a different career path. Love does not have to be weak and power does not have to be heartless.

Leaders who show love in their leadership will go out of their way to ensure that their colleagues feel valued, trusted and understood. They are more likely to create a positive and happy culture. Love makes work relevant; it creates a climate for growth and learning, it brings people together and acknowledges their contribution.

 Prompts for personal reflection

- Quite often, it is fear that stops us leading with power and fear that holds us back from leading with love. What fears do you have about being a more powerful or a more loving leader? How can you use love to help you lead with more power and power to help you lead with more love?

- When have you needed to emphasise power in your leadership and when have you needed to emphasise love?

■ When you agree a course of action, stop and ask yourself, where is the power in this decision or action and where is the love? Is the balance right? When it is a particularly difficult decision, discuss this with a trusted colleague. Consider whether your power needs softening with love or whether your love needs toughening up with power.

Power and love in organisations

A fractal is a never-ending pattern that repeats itself at different scales. They can be found all over nature, as well as in geometry and algebra – anywhere we find the same pattern repeated again and again. For example, the tiny bifurcations of blood vessels and neurons, the branching of trees, lightning bolts and river networks, the spiral distribution of seeds in a sunflower or pinecone and the way that frost forms on your windshield in the winter all have a fractal element.

Margaret Wheatley (1994, p. 132) talks about the concept of a fractal organisation: 'The very best organizations have a fractal quality to them … There is a consistency and predictability to the quality of behavior.'

In organisations with a fractal quality, the way that people behave has 'pattern integrity'. This can be understood as the culture of the organisation or 'the way we do things around here'. Where there is a positive culture, the consistency and reliability of relationships generates trust and the pattern is replicated throughout every layer of the organisation. Everyone is connected, which creates feedback loops that permeate from top to bottom in the organisation. As a result, there is a strong and consistent flow of information, expectations, reciprocity, mutual regard and positive culture. Where there is a negative culture, the pattern effect leads to repeated negativity within the organisation, gossip chains which mean that information gets leaked or lost, and a sense of disconnectedness from the whole.

Imperfect leaders use power and love together to create an integrity in the way that people behave at every level of the organisation. The pattern they create (and replicate) can be seen in the extent to which each individual plays their part in achieving organisational goals through relentless determination, high expectations, high challenge and accountability, so that things get done and done well (power), and the extent to which people work together with others, collaboratively and in unity, where the culture of kindness, openness, humility and empathy allow for growth, reflection, learning and development (love).

 ## Prompt for personal reflection

▪ What are the patterns of behaviours in your team? Do you see both power and love manifested in their leadership? How can you challenge them to reflect balance in their approach?

Power and love in school improvement

Power and love are fundamental to change, growth and development. Greany (2018) and Gilbert (2017), both writing about school improvement in partnerships of schools, describe the key ingredients that support school improvement (see Figure 7.1).

At its most basic level, school improvement is about understanding the specific needs of the school, providing or brokering support to meet those needs, and then ensuring that there is strong accountability and challenge. In other words, leaders need to be powerful in their drive for improvement, ensuring absolute clarity about the things that need to get better and holding teachers and others to account for improvement. But, critically, they also need to ensure that the right support, development and guidance is in place. Power and love in action together create the right conditions for improvement.

Figure 7.1. School improvement fundamentals

Imperfect leaders know that using their power is critical to growth and improvement, but they combine this with love to create the conditions in which change and growth can occur. This is important for school leaders to hold on to, as too often the wider education system (like the inspection system) emphasises the accountability and challenge aspect.

Power and love in the wider education system

At national and state level, the balance between power and love is sometimes lacking. There is too often a much greater focus on power and a lot less on love. As Munby and Fullan (2016, p. 3) observe:

> Many of us have worked for years in systems which are caught in a struggle between … country-level policy on the one hand and the action or inaction of individual schools on the other. Policy pushes in one direction, the profession pulls in another. The result is a type of friction which produces heat but not light: plenty of activity but not enough systematic change or improvement in outcomes.

Cláudia Costin, when she was leader of education in Rio de Janeiro, said: 'You can only transform education together with the teachers.' She added: 'The speed was given by the capacity of having teachers on board. We challenged them to the limit, but not more than the limit' (Costin, 2014, quoted in Elwick and McAleavy, 2015). Costin knew that she had to move with pace and that children only get one chance at an education, but she also knew that she could only push so far without losing the teaching profession – and without their support the change wouldn't be successful. She led with power but also with love.

Too often, governments start out with a focus on the love side of leadership, perhaps wanting to be inclusive, but when their ideas and proposals meet with resistance (as is almost inevitable) they either revert to the power side and give up on the love aspect or they simply stop doing it and try another initiative. If change is to stick – in a school or across a whole education system – then there should be a balance between power and love in the leadership: driving change forward but also showing empathy and taking time to make sure there is a critical mass in support of the way forward.

Without a balance between power and love at government level, positive change at school and at classroom level is unlikely. Political leaders who are serious about implementing change might benefit from being slightly less certain that they are always right and, instead, embrace the concept of power and love in leadership.

In the following case study, Gillian Hamilton explains that by co-constructing the Scottish leadership development programmes with school leaders, rather than driving them through in a top-down way, there was more ownership of the programmes. She also describes how when she was appointed to one of the top education jobs in Scotland (CEO of the Scottish College for Educational Leadership), she had self-doubt and needed support and love from colleagues. But she refused to lower her expectations of what needed to be achieved (power), and at the same time she showed love and inclusivity in her leadership by co-constructing the leadership programmes alongside teachers and school leaders. This ultimately led to more effective leadership development programmes, as she tapped into a wealth of expertise in the system and built a sense of collective responsibility.

 Case study

Gillian Hamilton, strategic director, Education Scotland

From 2014 until 2018, I was the chief executive of the newly formed Scottish College for Educational Leadership (SCEL). This was a unique role. As it turned out, I was the only CEO to ever hold that position because in 2018 the roles and functions of SCEL moved to Education Scotland, the country's national education agency. Thankfully, the work we imagined and developed has continued to grow.

As a former teacher and school leader, I have always been convinced of the difference that high-quality leadership development makes to our profession and, ultimately, to our young people. Prior to establishing SCEL, I had been privileged to work locally and nationally in this field, as a quality improvement officer in East Ayrshire Council and as head of educational services at the General Teaching Council for Scotland.

From the moment I read recommendation 50 in Professor Graeme Donaldson's *Teaching Scotland's Future* report (2010, p. 101) – 'A virtual college of school leadership should be developed to improve leadership capacity at all levels within Scottish education' – I knew that the opportunity to lead that organisation was my dream role, and one that I would love. With my belief that great leadership development makes a difference, alongside my passion, experience and commitment to Scotland's young people, I submitted an application for the post.

You might think this next paragraph will be a fairy-tale ending, but actually – swiftly following a successful interview and a resulting phone call to offer me the job – what came was the dawning realisation that I may well have passion, commitment, experience in the field and a belief in the importance of leadership development, but not the first idea how to be a chief executive. I remember, amidst the messages and phone calls of congratulations, switching off my phone and heading to the cinema on my own, wondering what on earth I might do next. That was when self-doubt crept in. How could I possibly do this CEO role effectively when my experience of executive leadership at a national level was so limited?

And that is where power comes to the fore – not the power and influence of an individual leader but the power of relationships, networks and the ability to admit that you don't have all the answers.

In comparison to many other countries, Scotland has a fairly small education system, and I was really fortunate to have built strong relationships with colleagues in professional associations, employers, other national organisations and many existing school leaders in roles prior to moving to SCEL. Looking back, the power of those networks ensured that I had sounding boards: other chief executives who were leading other national organisations, school leaders who provided honest and challenging feedback about some of our early thinking and programmes, and leaders across local authorities and professional associations who were powerful advocates for our work.

This gave me, and in turn our growing team, the confidence to innovate – to experiment with different ideas and ways of working. We ran programmes as prototypes rather than finished articles, building them with and for teachers and school leaders and proactively seeking feedback from those networks I mentioned earlier. This meant that the programmes were really well-received by teachers and school leaders, and I continue to be humbled when I hear previous participants talk about the significant impact that engagement in these programmes had on their own development.

What did I learn? Well, that is what brings me to the love element. Right at the start of my career, I used to think that when I moved into different professional roles I would need to *be* someone different. I have told the story many times to aspiring school leaders about the hideous salmon-pink blazer that I purchased when I was starting my very first leadership role. I thought I needed to behave differently, to be different as a leader, and I purchased a (hideous) pink blazer to wear to work. I quickly realised that, actually, to be the best leader I could be, I needed to be me and not an impersonation of some abstract leader.

As chief executive, I know that I had the power to influence aspiring and existing school leaders, and at every opportunity I tried to model that authentic leadership – by turning up as myself, by admitting that I didn't have all the answers, and that our teams, our young people and our nation would be best served by that approach. I have had the privilege of speaking to every new cohort of aspiring school leaders at the launch of the Into Headship programme, Scotland's national qualification for school leaders. Although the context may change each year, I always include reference to the strong moral purpose that is so evident in our teachers, the power of networks and asking for help, and, hopefully, I inspire our school leaders to lead as themselves.

The Scottish Government's National Performance Framework includes a commitment that Scotland's young people should 'grow up loved, safe and respected so that [they] realise [their] full potential'.[1] Scotland's teachers and school leaders, with the strong moral purpose that I referenced earlier, play a vital part in that.

One of the national leaders who is most admired at the moment is Jacinda Ardern, the prime minister of New Zealand. She seems to embody a great balance between power and love in her leadership. She is making important decisions during the pandemic but, so far, seems to be taking most of the citizens of New Zealand with her.

---

1   See https://nationalperformance.gov.scot/national-outcomes/children-and-young-people.

> ❝ One of the criticisms that I have faced over the years is that I'm not aggressive enough or assertive enough, or maybe somehow, because I'm empathetic, I'm weak. I totally rebel against that. I refuse to believe that you cannot be both compassionate and strong. (Jacinda Ardern quoted in Dowd, 2018)

So, have we got the balance right in our leadership? It is often a dilemma. Should we emphasise being decisive and strong, leading with authority and driving things through at pace? Do we nail our colours to the mast and step out in front and say, 'This way – follow me – now', or is now the time in our leadership to be more inclusive and empowering? Do we need to develop radical ways of operating and seize the moment to make an even bigger difference, or is it time for calmness, kindness and a sense of perspective?

There is an Old African proverb: 'If you want to walk fast, walk alone. If you want to walk far, walk together.' The dilemma for leaders is that we want both. Children only get a certain number of years at school, and therefore we cannot wait a few years before gradually bringing in the necessary improvements. We may need to move fast, so sometimes it may feel lonely as we are driving change through. But we will only have the ability to ensure lasting, long-term improvements in our organisations if we collaborate, show love in our leadership and walk together with others.

Summary

7

Power and Love

Without the balance between power and love in our leadership we may be heading for mediocrity and our organisation may get stuck, or we may be heading for quick fixes and people leaving because they don't feel valued. With a balance of power and love we can achieve great things.

Power

▧ Set high expectations of students and adults.

▧ Demonstrate drive and relentless focus. Refuse to be sidetracked from the most important things.

▧ Challenge complacency. Walk into the wind.

Love

▧ Co-construct the strategy. Build ownership.

▧ Demonstrate kindness and empathy.

▧ Be close to the climate and emotions of the organisation.

▧ Build long-term sustainable cultures.

 ## Exercises to try

▧ When you are facing a difficult conversation, or when you are wrestling with a challenge in your school or in your leadership, take some time to explicitly reflect on power and love. Divide a page into two halves and write 'power' on one side and 'love' on the other. Use this to record your responses to the questions below.

   » Where is the power in this situation? What is it that needs to be achieved? What is the goal?

   » Where is courage needed to walk into the wind?

   » Where is the love in this situation? Where do we need to better connect with those we lead?

» Whose voices do we need to hear? Where is compassion needed?

» What are the needs and desires of those around us (as well as our own)?

Use this to help you plan how to move forwards in that difficult conversation or challenging situation. Try to use power and love together in balance.

Spend some time with your leadership team reviewing whether, as a team, you have shown the right balance of power and love in recent months. Is the organisation feeling the power side or the love side from the leadership team at the moment? What might need to change as you move forward?

Chapter 8
Developing Future Leaders

Leadership and learning are indispensable to each other.

John F. Kennedy

Imperfect leaders encourage others to step up to leadership.

In Chapter 6, we focused on why imperfect leaders are restless learners. If we have an imperfect leadership mindset we know that, even if we have been a leader for a long time, we are still learning and able to improve and develop our leadership. This also means that we recognise leadership in others, even when it is embryonic or uncrafted, and we encourage others to step into leadership roles. We see potential in those around us to become the leaders of the future, and we seize the opportunity to invite others to begin their leadership journey as imperfect leaders too. We don't wait for perfection before giving colleagues opportunities to lead; we create learning organisations which bring the best out in others.

Developing future leaders takes time and intentionality

We all know how important it is for our own schools, and for the wider education system, to inspire and motivate others to become leaders. Many of us are good at talking the talk about developing future leaders, and we know what we should be doing, but sometimes it falls off the list. Perhaps the opportunity to develop others passes us by because we are so busy dealing with the urgent things on our list. Or, possibly (if we can admit it), we like to dominate the leadership space and find it hard to share the platform. There are lots of reasons why we might not develop future leaders as well as we could. Imperfect leaders know this, and so they proactively plan for how to make the development of future leaders a central part of their role rather than just vaguely hoping that it happens.

 ## Marie-Claire

In 2014, I gathered leaders within the KYRA Teaching School Alliance in Lincolnshire together to identify what our shared priorities were as a group of schools. One of the things that emerged was the need to systematically develop future leaders in ways that went beyond the traditional professional development programmes and courses. Head teachers in the alliance recognised that one of the factors that supported leadership development was a range of experiences and opportunities to learn and lead in a variety of contexts, alongside encouragement and feedback from someone more senior. The outcome was the development of the KYRA Leadership Matrix, a document designed to capture and make visible the variety of leadership experiences, opportunities and training future to which leaders in the KYRA alliance could have access, across and between the diverse schools in the partnership. The matrix included a range of options, including what a newly qualified teacher could do to develop their knowledge and experience of leadership (which might be around observing leadership meetings, leading part of a staff meeting or even just leading a whole-school assembly), through to what a head teacher could do to continually grow and develop themselves (for example, through peer review, school-to-school support and secondments to schools operating in other contexts). This tool has been used in many of the KYRA schools, with school leaders encouraging teachers to identify between one and three things they want to do each year to broaden and deepen their experience and learning.

Prompt for personal reflection

▪ What are the opportunities and barriers that get in the way when it comes to working with other local schools to develop future leaders together, and how might they be overcome (e.g. secondments, joint leadership development, job swaps)?

A tap on the shoulder

How do we encourage and support colleagues to step up into leadership? We think one of the first steps is to talk positively about leadership and the privilege of being trusted and given responsibility for doing a job that can have a profound influence on the life chances of children and young people. Being a school leader is a challenging job but it is also highly rewarding. At times, we might overemphasise the challenges and forget to talk about the positives. Secondly, there is nothing more powerful than a tap on the shoulder – someone seeking you out and saying, 'You could be a leader too.' However, this is just the start. There is much more we can do to support future leaders.

In the case study that follows, Sue Belton describes what it feels like to be tapped on the shoulder and the profound influence it has had on her. As an imperfect early career teacher, she felt humbled and unworthy of being given the opportunity, but it transformed her view of leadership. She has gone on to develop leader after leader through intentional talent-spotting and development, with a clear moral purpose about her role to 'grow talented leaders for all our schools'.

🔍 Case study

Sue Belton, head teacher, St Helena's Church of England Primary School, East Lindsey, England

I have been privileged to be the head teacher at St Helena's Primary School for the last twenty years; it is a voluntary-controlled church school in an isolated rural setting in East Lindsey, Lincolnshire, one of the poorest wards in the county and nineteenth poorest in the UK. We have 136 children on roll.

There have been many influences on me as a developing leader (I am still at that stage after thirty-eight years in the profession), but here are some of the critical, game-changing ones:

- The first head teacher I ever worked for, Gary Yates, asked me, of all people – a newly qualified teacher – to lead a staff meeting. How could I? I had nothing of significance to share with this talented team to whom I felt privileged to stand alongside. How clever he was; he saw something in me that I couldn't. I vowed then that if I was ever in the position of leading a school, I would give newly qualified teachers the nourishing roots to become a great teacher and then the nurturing push to lead and inspire others, even at the very beginning of their career.

- When working with teachers in Macedonia as part of a United Nations Children's Fund teacher training programme, I learned about the power of helping children to create beautiful outcomes amongst the rubble of conflict and loss. I returned home promising myself that I would never moan about resources, buildings, furniture and fittings again – it is all about human contact, relationships and authentic engagement.

- Listening to David Hargreaves call leaders to action our collective moral purpose (see Hargreaves, 2010), I knew immediately that being successful in our own little school was not enough, was not right and created a ceiling on its capacity to improve. I needed to reach out; I was not enough for our school on my own.

All of these experiences have made me realise that no school is an island, that no leader is enough on their own, and that building collective moral purpose and developing future leaders is the legacy I want to leave.

I am proud of our small village school and its commitment to growing our own talented leaders at all levels. My role as head teacher is to ensure that everything I do enables the staff to grow, to feel empowered, to feel valued, and to dream big for the children and for themselves. I believe that every person employed in my school has hidden leadership talents, and it is my job to find them and help them use them.

Our termly appraisal discussions begin by finding out what in the learning and teaching must be praised (the word is embedded in the process name for a reason) and celebrated, what can be learned from this, what needs to be shared with others, who could help to refine it further and what next. During our appraisal conversations, we refer to the KYRA Leadership Matrix – a framework which outlines all of the key opportunities, activities and professional development that teachers and leaders can engage in within and beyond our school to develop their leadership skills, knowledge and behaviours. This document is used as a scaffold in the conversation. Right from the moment a new team member joins our school, be they a newly qualified or recently qualified teacher, teaching assistant or highly experienced practitioner, we talk about leadership.

At the surface level, this matrix may seem like an endless list of tasks, but the key is the unfolding conversation with a colleague, during which we talk about leadership qualities and experiences and how together we can develop leadership in all of us. The matrix encourages forward thinking, action planning ('dreaming and scheming' as we call it in school), self-motivation, and a personal control and thirst for continuing professional development.

Trusting relationships are implicit within this process; I absolutely trust that all staff will do their very best to ensure their leadership roles are fulfilled and their actions are in the best interests of all the children in school. In return, they know they can be brave and bold in their plans, experimenting and exploring new ideas, projects, resources and research. They know they will have my utmost support.

There is no need for scrutiny; there is absolute need for honesty, vulnerability and openness.

I have been very fortunate to build several teams over the twenty years I have remained at St Helena's, and one of my defining mantras is to never hold on to a flourishing colleague too tightly (although there have been many times when I have wanted to). I believe head teachers have a collective moral responsibility to grow talented leaders for all our schools, and one of the things that gives me the greatest satisfaction is to have a teacher leave for a leadership role in a local school.

I will often seize the chance for a colleague to take up a seconded leadership role, even though it will leave an immediate gaping hole in our school setting. Almost every time I have agreed to this, the colleague has not returned; they have grown into their new role quickly, buoyed by immense support, and the substantive position has followed. At the time, they would have said they were not ready for such dizzy heights – but honestly, is anyone?

I remember employing a newly qualified teacher, who in a previous world had managed and led an international marketing company but had always wanted to teach. From the day of her interview, it was clear she was an outstanding practitioner, communicator and creative thinker, someone we would all aspire to be like. I knew then that my role in her career, and my aim for the greater good of education in our locality, was to fast-track her into headship. As much as I wanted to keep her at our school forever, she was destined to lead her own setting. I did everything to help her build her self-confidence and acknowledge her talents.

Within three years, a secondment arose for an acting headship. We talked it through. I assured her that she didn't need to set the school's budget on her own – that our school business manager had all the knowledge she needed for that. I assured her that there would be plenty of mentors to support her if she wanted them. After hours of reassuring her that she was totally ready for the role and that she should dare to have a go, she reluctantly agreed. That school never looked back, trebled in size and she has since become a beacon of support for many head teachers in the county.

Prompts for personal reflection

- Who encouraged you as a young leader? What did they do that helped you, inspired you or motivated you?

- Who are you helping, inspiring and motivating now? Who are the leaders you are actively developing in your school?

- Are there any future leaders who would benefit from a tap on the shoulder and an encouragement to consider leadership?

Leadership development

The role of a teacher is to help children and young people learn and develop. This is also the role of a leader, but leaders are responsible for the learning and development of all the adults in the school, as well as the students. In some ways, developing teaching practice is more straightforward than developing leadership practice. We know what the components of developing great teaching look like. We observe what is going on in the classroom, support teachers with clear instructional coaching and feedback, and then give them the opportunity to refine their practice, observe others and improve incrementally. We can also use student progress and outcomes to make a judgement about the effectiveness of teaching over time.

But if we want to develop great leadership, what do we do? How do we watch someone lead? Do we observe someone chairing a meeting or holding a conversation? Do we witness a leader walking around the school or dealing with a parent? Can we observe them grappling with a decision about the curriculum, or with the wording of a difficult email? It is much harder to capture. Leadership is the sum of many parts, actions, thoughts and decisions. It can be hard to get at!

The National College for School Leadership in England (see Munby, 2020a) concluded that effective leadership development needed five things:

1. **Learning on the job.** The main way we learn how to teach is by teaching, and the main way we learn how to lead is by leading. Listening to experts speak and reading case studies and research evidence is important but not sufficient.

2. **Focused feedback from credible peers, mentors or coaches.** Like Ericsson's deliberate practice cycle, leaders try out a new and specific technique, receive feedback on whether or not it worked and adjust their practice in light of the feedback (Ericsson et al., 1993).

3. **Exposure to outstanding practice in other contexts.** We need to make sure that we are not simply recycling mediocre practice because that is all we know. We therefore need to be exposed to exceptional leadership elsewhere, otherwise our expectations may be too low.

4. **Access to high-quality research, case studies and materials.** The content and domain-specific knowledge aspects of school leadership have to be strong. We need to ensure that leaders who step up into more senior roles further develop the expert knowledge and understanding they need in order to lead a school (compared to, for example, leading a hospital or a small business). School leaders with weak knowledge of school improvement and who don't know what a coherent curriculum or great teaching and learning looks like, are likely to be ineffective. It is not just about development of the more generic leadership skills, such as relationship-building, fostering an open culture, communicating effectively and holding challenging conversations. The domain-specific aspects of leadership also matter a great deal.

5. **Time for reflection and discussion with peers.** Sharing ideas, learning from each other and building support networks.

Without all five of these aspects, effective leadership behaviours are unlikely to become embedded into habits.

Rather than relying solely on external leadership development programmes to nurture the leaders in our organisation (excellent though they may be), it is important that we establish a culture that encourages improvement, supports risk-taking and learning in leadership, and gives opportunities to future leaders to try things out and reflect on their leadership. Embracing an imperfect leadership mindset means that when we develop other leaders, we create space for them to learn and make mistakes, to get meaningful feedback, to develop knowledge and understanding from other contexts, and to build reflection into the process. We also open up our own imperfect leadership for others to learn from.

 ## Marie-Claire

One of the first things I did when I became a head teacher was set up a shared leadership office with two spare desks at which a deputy or assistant head teacher (or even middle leader) could work. This was a deliberate way of opening up my leadership practice so that my senior colleagues could work closely with me and observe how I worked. I have repeated it in every school I have led. It has provided me with the opportunity to frequently invite colleagues to share the leadership space, shadow me, and pick up leadership tasks and opportunities to develop as they arose. I called it micro-learning.

For example, when the administrator put through a call from a concerned parent, when appropriate, I would invite my deputy or assistant head teacher to listen in, and then we would discuss how I had handled it afterwards. At times, I would delegate the call to them, and I would listen in and give them feedback afterwards. Because we were in a shared space, I was also much more likely to ask, 'Can I just run this past you?' and use the opportunity to grapple with difficult decisions together. I would try to model that as the leader it was okay to say, 'I don't know – let me get back to you,' so I could buy myself some thinking time.

It was also important to ensure that the leadership space was a safe space and open to all members of the staff team to come and talk to me as the head teacher. A shared leadership office has to be managed very carefully so as not to portray an 'us and them' environment or limit people from seeking you out as a leader. Five senior leaders who shared an office with me have since moved on to become head teachers in their own right, and many of them also have shared office spaces for micro-learning.

Delegation

Distributing leadership (or delegation) can be demanding and challenging for school leaders. But we believe it is an effective way of developing leadership capacity and capability in our schools and organisations – and a great way of developing future leaders. It is not as simple as just creating a list of what we want other people in the organisation to do. As the person ultimately in charge, we need to have confidence in the people to whom we are delegating and learn how to support them, as well as explore our own corresponding leadership change (i.e. what we are now not doing). We need to be very clear about what can be delegated and what cannot, as well as how we will manage psychologically when the buck doesn't get passed back up the leadership chain to us or when things go wrong.

It can also be challenging for those you lead when you make a shift towards a more distributed model of leadership. Making changes can interfere with established leadership dynamics and create a feeling of upheaval as expectations shift and your colleagues adjust. We believe the key is ensuring that you provide the organisational glue that holds everyone together and keeps the core focus on learning outcomes. Colleagues need to know how you will support and challenge other leaders in the organisation, that you are not abdicating responsibility and that no one needs to be perfect.

We have come across some leaders who can be overprotective of their colleagues and who choose not to delegate some of the harder things in leadership to their team. There are five reasons why senior leaders tend not to delegate the really hard aspects of leadership to colleagues:

1. **Risk.** The issue is mission critical for the school and we think that it is too high risk to let mistakes happen.

2. **Expectations of others.** Parents, external stakeholders, and staff, for example, might expect this task to be done by the head teacher.

3. **Expertise.** We think we know more about the issue than the team member and it would take too long to change that.

4. **Workload.** We feel that our team members are working as hard as they possibly can and we want to protect them. Since we are paid more, we should take the extra responsibility and workload upon ourselves.

5. **Control.** We like control and feel uncomfortable giving some of it away, even though we may know it is the right thing to do in principle.

We think that it is worth reflecting on this list. There is a fine line between protecting our staff and disempowering our staff. If we are serious about developing leaders, then they should get a chance to lead in the high-stakes and really difficult moments too. How will they learn these things if they are never given the opportunity to do them? Few things in a school are mission critical. Expectations from parents and staff can be changed over time. If we don't invest in passing on our expertise, we will be building in an over-reliance on us as an individual and thus helping to create a single point of failure if we are not around. Those with an imperfect leadership mindset are less likely to feel the need to control everything themselves, and because they know they don't know it all and they remember how they learned from their own mistakes, they don't expect their team members to know it all either. Instead, they provide structured opportunities to help their team members to learn and develop.

We believe that aspirant leaders should be provided with challenging opportunities and responsibilities, with support and feedback, such as handling a complex staffing issue, chairing a problematic meeting with unhappy parents or fronting a formal and high-profile event. If our colleagues are not given a chance to try these kinds of tasks, how are they going to be equipped to be leaders in the future?

 Steve

The National College for School Leadership always held an annual conference for new head teachers. This big event in London brought together over 400 new heads every year. It was expected by the stakeholders that, as CEO, I would do a keynote speech at this event. I did so for the first five years in the job. To be honest, making speeches is one of my strengths as a leader. But I found myself talking in my speeches about the importance of developing other leaders and then failing to do so myself. How were my senior colleagues going to learn the skill of making a keynote speech at a high-profile event unless they were given the chance to do it themselves? So, in my sixth year my then deputy made the keynote speech, and in my seventh my new deputy made the keynote speech. I supported them from behind the scenes. Both keynotes were very well received and the stakeholders soon shifted their expectation that it had to be the CEO who made the speeches. Incidentally, both of those deputies went on to be CEOs themselves.

 Prompt for personal reflection

▧ What is the most challenging aspect of your current leadership role? And what part of your leadership role do you love and are very good at? Consider whether you could safely hand either of these over to another leader in your school for their development. What would you need to put in place to support them? How would you give them feedback?

Gate-keeper or gate-blocker

We have sometimes come across school leaders who are quick to find reasons why people aren't ready for senior leadership. They feel that colleagues have to serve their time and only after they have experienced every aspect of school leadership, and shown themselves to be fully expert in them all, are they finally encouraged to take on a headship role. Of course, experience and expertise in a range of senior roles can be extremely helpful in preparing for school headship, but the truth is that nobody is ever completely ready for their next leadership role. It is always a shock. It is never comfortable when you make that step up. (In fact, if you do find the first six months or so in a leadership role comfortable, then there is probably something wrong!) Imperfect leaders don't hold people back waiting for them to be perfect. They know when their colleagues are ready for a new challenge and then they encourage them to have a go. They give them time to develop and the support they need to succeed.

Steve

Many years ago, I was appointed to a new leadership role as an assistant director in a local education authority. This was a big step up for me. My role included overall responsibility for school improvement in all of the schools in the local authority, but it also included responsibility for the support of school governors and school boards, the development of lifelong learning opportunities for the citizens of the area, the management of youth services and study centres for young people, support for early years units and nursery schools, and even responsibility for developing access to employment. It was a much wider brief than I had ever experienced before, and I really struggled in my first six months in the role.

I was not doing the job well and felt that I was letting everyone down, so I decided to go and see my boss (the director) and offer my resignation. During that conversation my boss, Mark, had my future career in the palm of his hand. He could have accepted my resignation. He could have decided to cut his losses and try to find someone with wider experience to replace me; he must have noticed that I was struggling and not doing everything I was supposed to be doing. Instead, he said, 'Resignation not accepted.' He then put in quite a bit more support for me, which I appreciated greatly. I ended up being very effective in that role – indeed, I excelled at it. When my confidence was low in those early months, what I needed from my boss was additional support and also belief in me, and that is what I received.

Sadly, we have encountered schools where there is little or no leadership movement at middle or senior leadership level. All the leadership roles are taken, and therefore ambitious new teachers find there is no room for new leaders. We think it is important to keep things moving and create change and fluidity so that leaders don't become stagnant. If you notice that your middle and senior leaders are stable and settled, consider how to create secondments to other schools to give colleagues new learning opportunities whilst creating space for others to 'act up'. Alternatively, consider how to use honorariums to create short-term leadership responsibilities.

The poem 'Come to the edge' by Christopher Logue (1969) encapsulates the role of leaders in developing other leaders:

> Come to the edge.
> We might fall.
> Come to the edge.
> It's too high!
> COME TO THE EDGE!
> And they came
> and he pushed
> And they flew …

Imperfect leaders encourage others to step up and give them the confidence that they can do it. Because they have self-awareness, and they know themselves to be imperfect, they are clear that nobody is the finished product.

Leadership diversity

One of the easy traps to fall into when we are looking for future leadership talent in our school and organisations is bias, often unconscious bias. Too often we focus on the people we like, people with similar skills and expertise to ourselves, people who look the same as us, people who think the same as us; and in doing so we overlook potential. There is still no question that in the UK we do not have a diverse enough field for senior leadership positions in our schools. Some schools and organisations use a talent management framework to help to combat unconscious bias. Others make use of a wide range of different perspectives on talent within the organisation rather than relying solely on the views of the line manager. Imperfect leaders seek the views of others in the organisation, realising that they will have their own hidden bias and are open to challenge and change. They make diverse appointments and encourage diverse thinking.

Prompts for personal reflection

- Consider how well you know your emerging leaders. Who are you noticing and not noticing? What assumptions might you be holding about some of the potential leaders?

- When and how can you create space for developing future leaders to safely and confidently challenge organisational assumptions?

Not all leaders are the same

When you reflect on the members of your senior leadership team, you will recognise that each member is different and will have varied development needs. They will need encouragement, confidence and support, but in different ways. Some will be more like you, with similar skills and attitudes, and others will be quite unlike you. But they might all have the potential to be effective school head teachers or CEOs. Leadership requires expertise and skills that can be learned, but it doesn't require a particular personality type. There are highly effective extrovert leaders and highly effective introvert leaders.

 Marie-Claire

My first leadership opportunity came when I was in my fifth year of teaching when I was asked to be the ICT coordinator. Although I would describe myself as an introvert, I was technically minded, IT savvy and I enjoyed teaching ICT (as it was called at the time). My first task was to replace the IT suite with new computers and set up a new network. The bit of the role that I was most nervous about was leading the planned series of six staff training twilights on the new suite of computers. I loved teaching 5–6-year-olds, but I wasn't sure I was going to be able to teach my colleagues! I remember talking with the head teacher at the time and confessing that I didn't feel confident at all, that I was very happy doing the behind-the-scenes management tasks but the upfront stuff would be best led by someone else. Thankfully she didn't let me off the hook. She asked me what I needed from her and she coached me through what I could do to help myself.

In the end, I reverted back to what I did as a newly qualified teacher. I wrote a detailed lesson plan for each training session and made my colleagues a workbook with step-by-step instructions and photos to guide them (and guide me). I rehearsed a script, paying particular attention to what I was going to say in the first five minutes of the training (when I knew I would be at my most nervous). I ensured that all the IT was working. And, critically, the head teacher allowed me time to run through it all with her. The first session went really well, but instead of just patting me on the back and saying 'Well done', the head teacher gave me some very specific feedback which helped to build my confidence. To the outsider I looked like I was confident, extrovert and thriving in the role, but my head teacher knew that I needed some specific encouragement and feedback to do well.

Consider Figure 6.1 (see page 123) again about being grown-up and restless. How can we help those we lead to move towards or continue to be in that top right-hand quadrant?

If we treat our budding leaders just as workhorses, they will eventually get fed up and go elsewhere. They have great potential and enthusiasm, but they are inexperienced and may well make errors or mess up. As imperfect leaders, we remember all the mistakes we made as we developed as leaders, and we also remember how much we learned from those mistakes. We need to give people a chance to lead; to invest in their development and support; to create an environment and culture where it is okay to take some risks, with help. We need to consider how we might take a step back sometimes in order to enable others to step up.

If we want our experienced leaders to retain their restlessness, we need to consider what more we can do to energise and, on occasion, re-energise them. Most experienced leaders who have lost their motivation and are not performing well were good at their jobs once. Perhaps there is something going on in their personal life that is temporarily detracting from their ability to do their job? Perhaps they need a new challenge that will make them think and remind them why they enjoy their job? Perhaps that older leader on your team whom you currently perceive as a problem might, with the right new challenge, become part of the solution? Can you create new roles and opportunities that will enthuse them?

 ## Steve

Sometimes in my leadership I have been quick to push a senior colleague out of the organisation if I have felt that he or she did not have the skill set required for the future. At other times, I have perhaps been too slow to do so. It is always hard to get this right. One of the aspects of leadership that I have struggled with over the years, but have occasionally had significant success with, is how to engage and reinvigorate a senior leader who is feeling ground down or whose expertise is not being used as much as it might be.

Some of you may already be familiar with Jim Collins' (2017) point about the importance of getting the right people in the right seats on the bus. At times, rather than consider carefully how to move people to different seats, I have perhaps been too hasty to push them off the bus! At other times, I have found that changing the seating arrangements or creating a new role that is more suited to the skills and expertise of the individual concerned and/or provides them with a new challenge has worked wonders.

Prompts for personal reflection

▪ Think proactively about ways to re-energise long-standing leaders in your organisation and make better use of their expertise and interests to develop others. Talk to them about their passions and interests, and create space for them to innovate and undertake new leadership challenges.

▪ Work with your senior team to create a list of opportunities for other emerging leaders to shadow or participate in leadership work. How can you open up your leadership for others to get close to, observe and learn from?

Next-generation catalyst

Schools around the world are welcoming the arrival of new generations of post-millennial teachers who are our future leaders from Generation (or Gen) Z – employees born between 1997 and 2010. Researchers undertaking a global survey have found that becoming a leader is important to 61% of Gen Z, which is higher than the percentage of Gen Y (57%) (Bresman and Rao, 2017). We also know from the research that Gen Z are enthusiastic about the coaching and mentoring they might receive as a new leader, but cite a desire for significant levels of responsibility and more freedom as amongst the things that would attract them to leadership (Schwieger and Ladwig, 2018). In terms of retention, 75% of Gen Z would be interested in working for an organisation in which they could have multiple roles and opportunities within one place of employment (Fromm, 2018). How can we create multiple opportunities for development, growth and leadership in our schools? How can we become more fluid in the way we think about leadership development? How do we give the right levels of responsibility and freedom to our future and emerging leaders so that we can grow more leaders who, despite their imperfections, can thrive in an imperfect world?

Summary

One of our core roles as leaders is to enable our colleagues to grow and develop:

- Because we know we are imperfect, we don't expect our colleagues to be completely ready for leadership, so we encourage them (with a tap on the shoulder) and help to build their confidence.

- We recognise the importance of designing and creating opportunities within the school to support the development of colleagues.

- We need to try to avoid bias in how we identify talent and take steps to challenge our own assumptions.

How might school leaders support others to step up into a bigger leadership role?

- Model and articulate. Don't make leadership a 'secret garden'. Talk about your leadership imperfections and how they are key to your leadership growth.

- Create opportunities for peer coaching and mentoring, focusing on an agreed area for improvement.

- Embed line management that is developmental and nuanced, based on the individual you are managing and their development needs.

- Build in opportunities for those in the school with particular expertise and technical knowledge (including yourself) to share that know-how with others in a proactive way.

- Ask your team to identify the things they fear or hate most about leadership (e.g. data analysis, designing a curriculum, safeguarding) and pair them with someone who can help them.

- Introduce 360° feedback to promote self-awareness and improvement (modelled by the head teacher).

- Provide opportunities for job shadowing or secondments, within and outside the school.

- Allow people to carry out more challenging leadership tasks, with support.

- Create a support group to provide dedicated time for discussion and social learning.

- Advertise and interview for a project or initiative which needs to be led over a set period of time (e.g. a year). If possible, link this to an honorarium. Move the successful candidate on to the leadership team as an associate for the period of the work.

 ## Exercise to try

- Make a list of all the teachers in your school and identify whether there is anyone who you think was previously struggling but is now flourishing under your leadership because you spotted their potential and talent, invested in them and developed them. Now think about who your successor might spot that you missed. What can you do to develop them? Who else might you be missing?

Chapter 9
Authenticity and Doing the Right Thing

What made them vulnerable made them beautiful.

Brené Brown

Imperfect leaders know themselves and are authentic.

The concept of authenticity is not new; in fact, it has its roots in ancient Greek philosophy. The phrase 'know thyself', which was inscribed in the forecourt of the Temple of Apollo at Delphi in the fourth century BCE, has influenced writers, poets, philosophers and thinkers ever since. It is thought that even Shakespeare drew inspiration from this with the famous line from *Hamlet*, 'to thine own self be true', speaking of authenticity and avoiding self-deception.

However, the concept of authentic leadership has really only emerged in the past century, with a significant increase in interest from academics and practitioners over the last twenty years. Writers on the subject have proposed a range of definitions of authentic leadership, but perhaps the one that resonates most with the concept of imperfect leadership is:

> those individuals who are deeply aware of how they think and behave and are perceived by others as being aware of their own and others' values/moral perspective, knowledge, and strengths; aware of the context in which they operate; and who are confident, hopeful, optimistic, resilient, and high on moral character. (Avolio et al., 2004, p. 4)

Much has been written about why it is important for leaders to become more authentic. Rob Goffee and Gareth Jones argue compellingly in *Why Should Anyone Be Led By You? What It Takes to Be an Authentic Leader* (2016) that people prefer to work for, and to be led by, authentic leaders. But there is also a deeper reason to be authentic. Research has shown that the more authentic people are, the more likely they are to be happy (Wood et al., 2008).

It is a mistake to think about authenticity as a binary choice; we can never be completely authentic or completely inauthentic. Knowing ourselves and remaining true to ourselves is a journey towards becoming more authentic.

We believe that to become more authentic leaders, firstly we need to know who we are and what matters to us. But it also means acting in accordance with that knowledge – for example, expressing what we really think and believe and by doing the right thing. A simple way of thinking about authenticity is the extent to which we (a) know ourselves, (b) cultivate self-awareness, (c) show the best version of ourselves and (d) try to do the right thing.

First and foremost, becoming authentic is about knowing and owning our thoughts, emotions, needs and wants, as well as our values. It is about understanding ourselves well. As imperfect leaders, we know what matters to us and we are comfortable, both with our imperfections and our strengths. However, the challenge of knowing ourself is a lifetime's work.

Imperfect leaders cultivate self-awareness – specifically about their thoughts, feelings, motives and values – as well as their preferences and ways of operating

We talked in detail in Chapter 1 about the importance of developing self-awareness as a leader, particularly in relation to the context in which you lead. When thinking about authenticity and doing the right thing, the level of self-awareness needed requires us to dig deep and examine ourselves on a regular basis. Sometimes others can help us to understand ourselves better. As Rhian Jones outlines in her case study on page 190, participation in a development programme helped her to understand that she was a creative person, and this emboldened her as a leader.

We believe that it is helpful to talk to trusted mentors or coaches, but time spent reflecting on our own is also useful. As we build a deeper understanding of who we are as people and as leaders, it is important to recognise and accept both the desirable and undesirable parts of ourselves with unbiased objectivity. It is also critical that we value truthfulness and openness in our closest relationships and allow others to hold up a mirror and help us reflect. We need others to support our assessments of ourselves, help us to process our thoughts and feelings, and challenge our bias towards ourselves.

 ## Marie-Claire

I continue to find new levels of self-awareness as a person and as a leader. I am increasingly aware of the things I know that I can do well, as well as what other members of my team are far better at than I am. I am also more aware of my quirky approaches, idiosyncrasies and particular preferences. My grandmother used to say that as a child I liked everything to be 'just so', meaning that I had my own clear idea of how I wanted everything around me to be. For example, I have always known that I like things to be presented well visually. I can spend hours making PowerPoints look smart or making sure both the content and the visual appearance of a report looks good. I was the same as a classroom teacher – I took real pride in my classroom displays.

I have never seen this as a weakness; in fact, I have always prided myself on my ability to make things look pretty! However, I had some feedback recently that really stopped me in my tracks and shifted my perspective. One of my colleagues was kind enough, and brave enough, to tell me that sometimes when I present something that looks slick and super well-presented, it can give the impression that there is no room for other people's contributions. Of course, I had no intention of limiting others and would really welcome them feeding into my ideas, but I was unaware of the unintended side effects of producing an overly complete and polished-looking document, when the aim was to involve other people. Now that I am more aware, I have been able to address this by presenting in ways that explicitly require others' input before the final tasks of making it all look smart.

Imperfect leaders show the best version of themselves

Those we lead want us to be authentic, but they also want us to bring the best version of ourselves to our leadership. As imperfect leaders, we know what our imperfections are. But we also know the kind of leader we want to be, and we are constantly working at becoming the best version of ourselves. According to social psychologist Roy Baumeister (2019), we will report feeling highly authentic and satisfied when the way others think of us matches up with how we want to be seen. However, there is a challenge with the concept of authenticity and a dilemma for leaders.

We like the concept of healthy authenticity. Being an authentic leader isn't about being a 'warts and all' leader or a 'this is who I am, take it or leave it' leader. We are aware that we are imperfect, but we don't necessarily want to display the very worst aspects of our personality or the behaviours that we are most ashamed of to the world. As Scott Barry Kaufman (2019) writes: 'getting in touch with your best selves and intentionally actualizing your most creative, and growth-oriented potentialities is a much more worthy goal than spending your entire life trying to find your one true self. In my view, there is such a thing as *healthy* authenticity.'

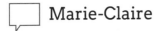 ## Marie-Claire

At times, I can become intimidated by the stories of leadership success shared on Twitter and other social media platforms. In many cases, there are genuine reasons to celebrate the achievements of other school leaders and applaud those who are doing incredible things. But I have to be honest and say that the stories that encourage me most are the ones where leaders have been able to authentically own not just their successes but also the challenges they have faced along the way and the things that haven't gone according to plan. Some might argue that Twitter isn't a place for leaders to admit these, and I agree that caution must be applied. But for that reason, it is important to remind ourselves that the stories of success we see on Twitter are a bit like some of the photos on Instagram – they may be authentic stories of success but filters have been applied and other aspects not shared at all. After all, most people tend to avoid posting photos of the messy bits of life.

Imperfect leaders develop healthy authenticity, recognising who we are as a whole person, taking responsibility for how we show up and working towards becoming the best version of ourselves.

Marie-Claire

Over the last few years, I have found a couple of tools and resources that have really helped me to find ways to show my authentic self. One is the Values in Action (VIA) Character Strengths self-assessment tool.[1] Alex Linley, a writer in this field, says that 'a strength is a pre-existing capacity for a particular way of behaving, thinking, or feeling that is authentic and energising to the user, and enables optimal functioning, development and performance' (Linley, 2008, p. 9). Research has correlated the active use and development of strengths with improved well-being, performance and resilience among other factors (Snyder and Lopez, 2009; Niemiec, 2012, 2020). When reviewing my strengths, I discovered that hope was in my top five.

For me, being authentic is about being hopeful and optimistic. It is about believing that there is a better future worth pursuing, that I have a contribution to make towards making things better for the children and young people we serve in education, and that despite obstacles, setbacks and challenges, better is always possible. When things are difficult and I fall into a mindset of hopelessness about situations or people, I know that I am not at my best and not being authentically me.

I have also become increasingly aware of my particular lens on the world – for example, the way in which I like to build connections between things, see patterns and possibilities, and create big-picture future-focused strategy. When I am leading that type of work, I am energised and at my most authentic. Recognising that I need others around me to show up with detail-focused implementation plans that help turn the big ideas into reality has helped me to build great teams and create space to be more authentically me, whilst helping others to be more authentically them.

---

1   This is available online and for free at www.viacharacter.org.

So, how do you know if you are being authentic? This great quote from an American psychologist and philosopher from the last century, William James, is helpful:

> I have often thought that the best way to define a man's character would be to seek out the particular mental or moral attitude in which, when it came upon him, he felt himself most deeply and intensively active and alive. At such moments, there is a voice inside which speaks and says, '*This* is the real me.' (James, 1920, p. 199)

 ## Prompts for personal reflection

- Take time to reflect on what energises you – when are you at your best or fully you?

- When do you think, 'This is the real me'?

- How might you show the best version of yourself more often?

Imperfect leaders try to do the right thing

The rhetoric–reality gap

Developing an imperfect leadership mindset means that we stay highly attuned to what can be described as the rhetoric–reality gap in our own leadership and in the organisations we lead. We know that trying to look good and disguising our mistakes undermines our authenticity. Imperfect leaders ensure that their actions match their words.

In 2017, security guards forcibly hauled a 69-year-old passenger from his seat on an American Airlines flight and dragged him off to find space for an additional crew member who needed to get to the destination. The passenger, Dr Dao, suffered a broken nose, concussion and lost two front teeth. Dr Dao had done nothing wrong. The official United Airlines slogan is 'Fly the Friendly Skies', yet, rather than looking after paying customers, on this occasion other priorities were seen to be more important (Bever, 2019).

In 2021, England's then minister for health, Matt Hancock, set out the rules on social distancing and urged the nation to keep to them, in spite of the hardship it caused, whilst he was conducting a clandestine affair that broke all the rules (Parkinson, 2021).

These instances of saying one thing and doing another are shocking, but not, alas, unique in the worlds of business and politics. Although we may be taken aback by these and other examples, it can be helpful to use them to reflect upon our own organisations and whether there is a rhetoric–reality gap there too, even if not such a glaring one.

Marie-Claire

I remember early in my teaching career being contacted by a friend who had just qualified and started her first job in a primary school. It was the day before October Census Day, and she rang me for advice. She said that the head teacher had called her into her office that morning to discuss a pupil who had been in her class at the start of the academic year but had recently left to move back to Egypt. The head teacher asked her to mark the pupil present in the paper register on Census Day, explaining that it would ensure the school received a little more funding in its budget that year. My friend was alarmed – she knew that what she was being asked to do was to falsify records and that it wasn't the right thing to do, but she also felt intimidated and scared of the head teacher and how she would respond if she said no to the request. We talked through the situation.

When we spoke later in the week, I asked her what she had decided to do. She had very courageously asked to see the head teacher the next morning and told her that she didn't feel comfortable with what she was being asked to do and that she would mark the pupil absent. She also said that if the head teacher wanted to alter the register, then that was on her conscience. Because she felt so exposed, she took photocopies of the register that day for her own records, just in case anything came back on her professionally. In the end, the head teacher didn't alter the register, but my friend had a very difficult term after that – the head teacher didn't speak to her for several weeks. It took real courage for her to act in line with her values. But what is important to note is that she knew what mattered to her long before she ended up in this situation: being authentic and true to herself and doing the right thing, even when under pressure.

We may have value statements hanging on our walls and an agreed mission statement, but how confident are we that these values are practised and genuinely inform the behaviour of everyone in the organisation? Viviane Robinson (2017) talks about the importance of virtues over values. Values, she argues, are important but theoretical. We become virtuous leaders if we apply those values in our daily behaviour at work. If we want to lead a virtuous organisation, which is true to its values, then there are two main ways to do this – modelling the behaviour and using systems and routines to incentivise it – and both are important.

Modelling

It would be great if you could create virtuous behaviour by making speeches and by putting up lists of values in the reception area of the school. Imperfect leaders don't hide behind vision statements and glossy brochures – they attend closely to their own leadership practice by modelling their values. As we have seen, imperfect leaders make mistakes, but if those mistakes are genuinely acknowledged and the same mistake isn't repeated regularly, then those we lead will understand. But, overall, it is up to us to model the behaviours we expect from others, so if there is a disconnect between our rhetoric and our own behaviours, then trust may be lost and there will be a negative impact on the culture.

Leaders inevitably, for good or bad and intentionally or unintentionally, cast a shadow or shed a light over their organisations. When you become a head teacher – the person who is ultimately in charge – you find that you are being watched as never before. Those who work for you and with you don't just listen to what you say, they spot what you don't say. If you praise one team or individual but forget to praise another team or individual, they will notice. Moreover, they don't just listen to your words, they watch your behaviours and your facial expressions. They even take notice of what clothes you wear.

You are modelling leadership and expectations, so a cross word, a grumpy look or a failure to smile at someone in the corridor can have a powerful negative impact. Equally, having a quiet word with a colleague if he or she is having a bad time or sending them a thoughtful card can have a really positive effect. Gradually, over time, your behaviours will have an impact on the culture of the organisation. If you regularly turn up late for meetings, then so will many of your colleagues; if you often look stressed or are irritable, then this behaviour will become more acceptable amongst your colleagues. 'Be the change you want to see' sounds trite but it turns out that, over time, it does have a big impact on organisations.

The culture of the organisation will also be influenced not only by what you choose to highlight but by what you choose to ignore. Lieutenant General David Morrison of the Australian Army responded to the announcement of a civilian police and defence investigation into allegations of unacceptable behaviour by army members, by stating in a powerful speech in 2013 that 'the standards we walk past are the standards we accept'. It is not just what we do, it is also what we don't do that can matter most here. Taking a clear stand, Morrison ensured that it was absolutely crystal clear that 'those who think that it is okay to behave in a way that demeans or exploits their colleagues have no place in this army'.[2]

We go to quite a lot of conferences where all staff from a group of schools or from a district or local authority attend together, and we have concluded that there are two types of CEOs or directors at these kinds of events. We see some CEOs or leaders of groups of schools (let's call them type 1 CEOs) arriving early, making a welcome speech at the beginning of the event, then staying for the whole day, circulating around the room, making sure they have spoken to everyone they can – a little word here, a little word there – and then standing at the door at the end thanking people for coming. We see other CEOs (type 2) who seem to think that once they have made their welcome speech, they can just disappear and go and do important work elsewhere. Alternatively, they do stay but spend the whole time chatting to just a small group of their friends and close colleagues.

The hidden message that type 2 CEOs are giving to their staff is that they don't matter, that they are not noticed and not valued. Type 1 CEOs are giving out a completely different message. They are saying: 'I am a learner too' and 'I am interested in what you do for the organisation.' We can forget sometimes how much it can matter to the people

---

2   See https://www.youtube.com/watch?v=dRQBtDtZTGA.

who work with us that we personally acknowledge the importance of their work. This is particularly true for more junior staff. Our behaviour as leaders is the most significant influence on the values and culture of the organisation, especially over time.

 ## Prompt for personal reflection

▢ If someone shadowed you for a week, what would they conclude from your behaviour about the culture you are modelling for the organisation?

Using systems and routines to incentivise virtuous behaviour

If we want to ensure that our organisations avoid the rhetoric–reality gap, modelling the behaviours we want to see is important but not sufficient. Our role as leaders isn't just to model the right kinds of behaviours; it is also to try to incentivise and institutionalise those behaviours.

People are smart, and they will tend to behave in the most appropriate way, given the circumstances in which they find themselves. If we find that a significant number of staff are behaving in a way that is not good for the culture of the organisation and are not modelling the values that we hope for, then the reason for this is likely to be connected with the organisation itself (or the external pressures being placed upon it), not individual members of staff.

 ## Steve

A few years ago, a head teacher at a primary school in England shared with me that she had a problem with attendance by the support staff during the last few days of each term (in England there are three terms a year). When we discussed this in more detail, it became clear that the incentives for support staff to take time off at the end of term when they were feeling a bit down or very tired, and to extend their holiday time, were greater than the incentives to turn up at work. People will tend to do the thing they are most incentivised to do, given the circumstances. Once the head teacher changed the incentives, strengthened the attendance policy and followed it up robustly, the problem mainly went away.

How we use our systems and routines to incentivise and institutionalise the right kinds of behaviour is important. This includes how we use school assemblies, parents' meetings, the recruitment and induction of new staff, performance management systems and our various human resources policies, and financial, health and safety systems. If we find that external pressures, such as the government's accountability system or pressures from parents and other stakeholders, are having a negative impact on the behaviour of the staff, leading to unethical or inappropriate conduct, then it is up to us to try to minimise or counteract those external pressures by creating internal systems that incentivise better behaviour.

 Steve

I remember many years ago when I worked in a local authority. One of my senior team was a likeable person who seemed enthusiastic and professional. When one of the finance officers said that she had some concerns about his budget, I was convinced that it would be nothing more than a minor glitch. But, of course, I told her to go ahead and investigate.

It turned out that this polite and professional member of my senior team had been paying his own mortgage from public funds for several years. I was shocked. He ended up in prison, and rightly so, but I had to ask myself, as a leader, how come the operating systems under my leadership weren't strong enough to prevent this happening, or to spot it more quickly? I had been so focused on the outward-facing aspect of the role – school improvement – that I had neglected to do enough to incentivise good internal financial management and to ensure that the systems and accountabilities were robust. My behaviours had unintended consequences. I became much more thorough in my approach to financial matters after that.

In the following case study, Carolyn Roberts describes a challenging day in her school. She models virtuous behaviour in very difficult circumstances in a deeply impressive and authentic way, as she is exposed to case after case of extremely difficult scenarios. One of the reasons she is able to cope with everything that comes at her is her strong sense of moral purpose and her commitment to doing the right thing. But, crucially, she is also able to come through this because she and her colleagues have invested a great deal of time in developing robust policies and systems that incentivise the right behaviours.

⌕ Case study

Carolyn Roberts, head teacher, Thomas Tallis School, London, England

I am the head teacher of a large mixed community comprehensive school in London. We have 2,000 students aged between 11 and 18, including 600 in the sixth form. I have been a head for twenty years; this is my third such post and at the time of writing I have been here for eight years.

When a big thing happens in school there is often time to reflect, discuss and take advice, but sometimes planned big things, ad hoc happenings and minor catastrophes clump together on one day. Knowing that this is normal doesn't help the feeling that some days are like an in-tray exercise designed by a malevolent lunatic.

Starting the day chairing a long-term planning meeting went well, but that was the high spot. Next, a permanent exclusion hearing was exacerbated by a tricky argument about cross-border fair access protocols.[3] Indoors, an allegation of racism was dealt with calmly, if lengthily, during the process. Outdoors, the excludee's friends and enemies fought in the yard and a teacher was injured. Waiting for the red mist to clear before statements could be taken meant that fixed-term exclusions had to wait until the next day.

One of the senior staff who usually handles such flare-ups was nowhere to be found. Why? Because she was dealing with a child whose mother had just died, unexpectedly, at home that morning. A child she knew well because of repeated suicide attempts. That meant the wash-up after the fight was led by another senior person whose knowledge of the boys, the background and the likely veracity of their accounts was very limited. That colleague excels in the classroom but he is not at his best with fights or random violence.

In another part of the school, Pride Week flags cause arguments. At the end of the day, a sixth-form student tells her head of year that a teacher said she should 'get over' sexist talk in class.

A parent swears at the cook and says that tap water is undrinkable. What am I going to do about it? Another parent swears at me when we resist our school being named as the most appropriate placement for a child with an education, health and care plan (EHCP) and tells me I am a disgrace to my profession. Another parent cries when she is served with an attendance notice. A head of year arrives agitated because a parent has told him she has complained about him to me, which she hasn't.

Left over from the day before: governors' disquiet over a budget deficit next year. Coming down the track tomorrow: an internal appointment that will generate gossip and a meeting with staff who won't get on together.

And, as the poet says, all day it has rained. The big indoor spaces are full of exams.

---

3   Fair access protocol agreements are designed to prevent children being permanently excluded from school by arranging a fair process for another school to take them on. In a crowded city, children often live across a local government administrative border. Sometimes the fair access processes don't talk to one another and a child has to be permanently excluded in order to get another school place.

Authenticity, to an extent, rests on temperament. This day needs a long view and a deep breath. It is not an unusual day, but it will require active navigation to avoid the many rocks.

The planning meeting went well because it was itself well-planned and the people around the table knew their roles and how to work together effectively. Completed, everyone went about their business efficiently. Time spent in the past on good job descriptions, on modelling pleasant relationships and on strict adherence to time boundaries facilitate success.

The permanent exclusion was upheld despite curveballs because the paperwork was in good order, the governors principled, kind and fair, and the allegation of racism unfounded – which we could prove by having the facts ready. The next skirmish in the cross-border fair access protocols battle can wait.

The bereaved child will have all the love we can give her – we know the older siblings and the family and have an excellent relationship with them all. We share in her grief and know what we will do next.

The fight wash-up leads to a row between colleagues after hours. They will regret it tomorrow when their deputy head lead will talk to them. The Pride Week flags are discussed by a patient tutor and reinstated. The sixth former will write down her thoughts and experiences overnight, and the head of year and I agree on some surveillance. I send a regretful email to the tap-water parent, who apologises. I grit my teeth over the EHCP and say ho-hum to myself over the attendance tears. The other parent is a vexatious complainer: comes with the territory.

We arrange a meeting of the deficit reduction group, and check with human resources that the internal appointment process will be transparent and scrutinisable. I happen to bump into some of the commentators and bid them a good evening. The warring faction will get a telling-off from mother tomorrow. The 350 lessons taught today have generally proceeded without incident. Stuff has been taught and learned, with laughter and frustration where appropriate. Everyone is a bit damp.

Authentic leadership calls for wisdom, experience, a commitment to justice, courage in the face of justifiable or ridiculous anger, and constant good humour. Some days run smoothly, but bad days only go well if you have put all of the structures in place on good days. You need to know and to model, in your own person, what you want colleagues to do and how you want them to be. And they should know what that it is because you tell them, often. Most of all, you should be calm.

School leaders are not just public servants but role models for children. Children deserve to see, every day, what it takes to live a good life, no matter what the weather brings.

 ## Steve

At the National College for School Leadership, every member of staff took part in 360° feedback annually. It was part of the performance management process. No matter what your role in the organisation, you could not do well and flourish at the National College if your colleagues did not believe that you were, on the whole, living the values of the organisation. We also highlighted different values each month and encouraged people to nominate colleagues to receive recognition for modelling that value. Later, when I was CEO of the Education Development Trust, all our annual awards for staff were based around exemplification and modelling of our core values. I found that these kinds of strategies helped to incentivise and embed the right values and behaviours in the organisation.

 ## Prompt for personal reflection

■ What systems and structures in your school hold the fabric of the school together, tuned into the culture you are trying to embody, and provide you with anchors as you grow as an imperfect and authentic leader?

Flexing our ethical muscles

Leaders in state schools are public servants. They are funded by the state to do the best they can to educate the children in their care and to implement the requirements placed upon them by the state. But within those parameters, they also have choices. They can decide to act in a way which is more ethical or less ethical. They can choose to reflect upon ethical grey areas and to flex their ethical muscles, or they can choose to make decisions which may help their career but which may not entirely sit well with their conscience or values.

In many education systems around the world, there are teacher shortages which can lead to competition between schools for staff. There is also competition for student places in many schools, and in most education systems there is an accountability approach from government that expects each school to do well in national tests or examinations. This can create real tensions between what is right for my school and what is right for our schools, between what is right for some children and what may seem to be in the best interests of the school.

In the following case study, Rhian Jones describes a moment in her own leadership when she realised that she had lost sight of her students as individuals and had come to view them as attainment levels: 'The external system had begun to bend me out of shape.' In spite of pressures to conform, she learned to flex her ethical muscles and to stand up for what was right.

 ## Case study

Rhian Jones, head teacher, Ysgol Y Faenol, Denbighshire, Wales

I began working in a primary school leadership role in 1999 and became a head teacher in 2008. I am someone who likes harmony and equilibrium. I like to conform and follow rules. I always strive to do my best; it matters to me what others think. I would describe myself as a dutiful school leader.

After I'd had a few years of headship experience and found my feet, I began to internally question the narrow, overburdened curriculum and high-stakes culture within which we were working. This initially led to a sense of dissatisfaction; an unease that I was part of a system which lacked breadth, seemed to stifle imagination and was at risk of losing the fun of learning. I saw staff and pupils showing increasing signs of stress from the external expectations placed upon them. My instinct was that, as a dutiful leader, I should somehow work harder to protect others from the stresses. Like many head teachers, I felt that I needed to problem-solve. I spent my time searching for ways in which we could improve our performance and work harder in our attempts to meet external expectations. My overriding worry was that if the school failed to meet the standards set out by the external system, that this would be a reflection on the quality of my leadership. This created an underlying level of pressure and stress.

The school where I was working had a large transient population, with new pupils arriving every couple of weeks. One day I realised, with horror, that I had stopped thinking of new arrivals as individuals, but had begun, on occasion, to view them as attainment levels. What had happened? The external system had begun to bend me out of shape. I was compliant in papering over the cracks and feeding into a system which overemphasised what was easily measurable rather than the whole child. I had fallen into the trap of chasing a silver bullet of school improvement. This wasn't what I wanted or what the children deserved. Surely, in my leadership role I needed to stand up for what was right – to be courageous and brave. My dilemma was how to balance this with my natural inclination to conform and be dutiful.

It was whilst I was agonising over this that I came across the creative habits of mind model (Lucas et al., 2013). This defines creativity as inquisitive, persistent, collaborative, disciplined and imaginative. I was quite intrigued by this model; it summed up what I believed that we, as educationalists, should facilitate for our learners. As I was reflecting upon this definition of creativity, it dawned on me that I am a creative person. It had never entered my head before that I was creative – I cannot sing or dance and have no sense of rhythm. I had spent my whole life lacking creative confidence. This new-found understanding of what creativity is was a revelation to me: wondering, questioning and challenging assumptions wasn't something negative but something I should be proud of; playing with possibilities, thinking outside the box and daring to be different was a strength; making connections and taking measured risks was positive.

The more I researched and looked into creative habits of mind, the more empowered I felt as a leader. This was the solution to my dilemma – I could do what was right and have confidence in what I believed. I didn't need to worry that others might think I was a difficult, awkward or uncooperative leader. Embracing these creative habits of mind emboldened me, both personally and as a leader. I felt freer and more willing to take risks. I could dare to be different! I was keen for those with whom I worked (both staff and pupils) to feel the same sense of confidence, inspiration and empowerment. Within our setting, we began to put creative habits of mind at the heart of what we do. My efforts to change my own mindset and the culture of the school hasn't been a quick fix. There are plenty of pitfalls and challenges along the way. Those external pressures are still there. I feel anxious at times about whether we are going in the right direction. Now, though, as a creative leader, I am more likely to respond to challenges with authenticity and enthusiasm, rather than dread and fear of failure.

Albert Einstein allegedly said, 'Creativity is contagious, pass it on.' In my experience it is hugely contagious! It empowers and emboldens. As I, and the others around me, have begun developing our creative habits of mind, there is a sense of excitement about learning and the future. When we refer to learners in our school, we include everyone. Adults, as well as children, are on a creative learning journey together. We embrace 'marvellous mistakes' and relish 'playing with possibilities'. Feedback from a teacher which encapsulates this change in culture is: 'You can try innovative teaching without fear. If things don't go as planned, we reflect as a team and work together to improve.' This sense of collaboration and teamwork has had a hugely positive impact upon well-being and learning. Teachers are slowly but steadily becoming more confident in being facilitators – promoting deep questioning and enquiry-based learning. Feedback from pupils in Years 5 and 6 shows the impact from a child's perspective: 'It's fun and exciting, more like free learning – our teacher gives us something to work towards and the freedom to do it.'

The move towards creativity has created a passion, a buzz of enthusiasm and eagerness. Embracing this has made me a bolder and braver leader. Ironically, as I have developed the confidence to stop chasing that high-stakes silver bullet of school improvement, the work of the school has been positively acknowledged by external agencies more than ever before.

Like Rhian, head teachers may find themselves with some challenging ethical issues to address. Consider these examples:

- Our school desperately needs a science teacher and I observe a great one during my recent visit to a local school. Do I go out of my way to persuade this talented science teacher to apply to our school when I know it will be great for us but have a negative impact on the school they may be leaving?

- A school nearby needs help. Do I keep my head down and focus on the many challenges in my own school or do I offer support?

- I genuinely want our school to be inclusive, but I know that by taking in challenging children from other schools we will probably do less well in terms of accountability measures. Should I refuse to take in more of these children?

- I find that we have some very difficult children in the school who are taking up a huge amount of our staff time and are unlikely to get good results in tests. My teachers are doing all they can but they are finding it very wearing. Do I try to persuade the parents to take them to a more 'suitable' school?

- Some of our students want to follow a curriculum pathway that would be well-suited for them but would not put the school in a good light in the government's accountability measures. Do I put the needs of those students first and risk damaging the reputation of the school?

A head teacher in England tells the story of how the parents of an 11-year-old boy were desperate to get their son into the school next door to hers, but they lost their appeal and the boy came to her school instead. The student was extremely bright and had strong parental support, so the chances of a whole string of good examination results was very high. However, the boy had a stunning singing voice and her school's music department didn't cater for choral singing, although the school next door did.

What did the head do? It was better for her school if the boy remained, but probably better for the child if he went to the neighbouring school. She wrote to the appeals panel and asked to get the boy admitted to the school next door. The head teacher was modelling principled decision-making in the interests of the child, not putting her school first. And the knock-on effect? The other heads she worked with began to behave in a more principled way themselves – towards student exchange and school admissions. Acts of kindness and principled leadership are not only good in themselves, they can have positive consequences for the system too.

Imperfect leaders struggle with these ethical issues. They want to do the right thing, but they know some of these are grey areas, are not clear-cut and require careful thought. They ask for advice from wise colleagues and mentors. They think through the consequences – long-term as well as immediate – of their decisions. They flex their ethical muscles. As Evelyn Forde outlines in the following powerful case study, when faced with shameful and unethical behaviour, authentic leaders choose not to ignore the issue; instead, in a calm and measured way, they choose to do the right thing.

 ## Case study

Evelyn Forde, MBE, head teacher, Copthall School, London, England, and vice-president, Association of School and College Leaders

I have been working in schools for over twenty years and as a head teacher for the past seven years. I have experienced all sorts of changes and challenges which have left me shaken, exasperated, curious and determined, all in equal measure. It is not always easy being a black female leader, but it is truly an honour and a privilege, and as such, I will always use my voice to champion diversity, inclusion and equality. The one key thing I learned during my time on a leadership programme in 2008 was to always be your authentic self.

I left school with no qualifications from an education system that failed to catch me or guide me. When I finally realised the value of education for myself, I was determined to make a difference for the young people we serve and the staff I would eventually lead. As a head, you are often made aware that 'the job isn't easy' and 'it's lonely at the top', but until you are there you don't realise how true these statements truly are.

Many a time as head teacher I have walked into conference halls and leadership seminars and looked around to find nobody that looked like me, or at the very most just one other. At first I found this quite disconcerting – and I say this because in all the schools in which I have worked (bar one) I have always served a very diverse community – so, to go to head teachers' conferences and see no other black head teachers, I used to think, where are the schools that they lead? But, at times like that, I always put my best foot forward. I would not shy away from introducing myself and being ever so proud of my school. After all, if I did anything other than that I would not be me; I would be trying to be someone else and that just wouldn't have worked.

A turning point for me during my time as head teacher was when I attended a leadership conference in 2019. At the evening gala meal, all very posh and lovely, I respectfully pointed out to a group of delegates that they were sitting at the table I had booked for my colleagues. I was told that, no, that couldn't be so as they had booked it. When challenged a little bit more by me, and I named my school and those of my colleagues, the delegate apologised and said, 'Sorry, I thought you worked here.' I just couldn't believe that in 2019 there was still this view that black people could not be head teachers. Yes, the statistics remain shockingly low – only 3% of head teachers in England are from a black, Asian and minority ethnic (BAME) background – but surely there isn't a widely held view that we cannot do the job.

Rather than let this stop me, rather than allow this to go unchallenged, I decided I needed to be in a position of some influence, a position that would shine a lens on the wonderful black and brown leaders who are out there, the wonderful black and brown teachers who are aspiring to become leaders, so that their experiences would hopefully be different to mine. I applied to become a council member for one of the largest professional leadership associations in the UK, the Association of School and College Leaders. I then put myself forward to chair their first BAME Leaders' Network as part of their equality, diversity and inclusion strategy. I then decided to apply to become the association's president in 2022–2023. In 2021, I will be the vice-president before taking up the position of president the following year.

The journey to headship, or any leadership position, is never easy and there will always be challenges that test you and make you stop, reflect and really question yourself, but that is no reason to give up. When I was faced with the question of my authenticity at the gala dinner, my immediate reaction was, 'How dare you?' but later I thought, actually, what is needed here is education and challenge. Challenge articulately, calmly and confidently, and educate in the hope that we will be able to remove the bias and ignorance.

A recent talk by Corinne Momal-Vanian, executive director of the Kofi Annan Foundation, included this quote from Sheryl Sandberg (2013): 'Leadership is about making others better as a result of your presence and making sure that impact lasts in your absence.' For me, I have learned as a leader that to make change happen, yes, you can be on the sidelines and support when you can, and, yes, you can be part of a grassroots movement and influence change. But, to begin to make structural changes in a system that, in my view, has been inherently biased and at times overtly racist, you need to get to the heart of policy-making and you need to sit at the same table as the decision-makers. I urge all leaders, though, when they get to that table, to remain your true authentic self. Remember the journey you have travelled and those who are travelling behind you, and always do the right thing by them and the children we serve – because if we don't, who will?

Evelyn decided to do the right thing, even though it was challenging. If you are still struggling with what is the right thing to do, here are four tests suggested by Marc Le Menestrel (2011):

1. **The sleeping test**: if I do this, can I sleep at night?

2. **The newspaper test**: would I still do this if it was published in a newspaper?

3. **The mirror test**: if I do this, can I feel comfortable looking at myself in the mirror?

4. **The teenager test**: would I mind my children knowing about this?

In the UK, there are seven principles of public life – known as the Nolan Principles. They were established in 1995 by the Committee on Standards in Public Life and apply to anyone holding public office. They are: selflessness, integrity, objectivity, accountability, openness, honesty and leadership (holders of public office should demonstrate these principles in their behaviour). They can help us to reflect on our own role and our own behaviours, even if not all our politicians keep to them.

 ## Prompts for personal reflection

- Are there any behaviour issues amongst your staff that you are walking past rather than confronting?
- Are there any examples in your leadership where you are doing what you think is expected of you rather than doing what you know is the right thing? Is it time to flex your ethical muscle?

Finally, we believe that trying to do the right thing and leading in an ethical way is essential not just for the staff but also for the students. The children and young people in our care will be watching how we and our colleagues behave. It is vital that we role model the values we promote and create an environment where young people can grow up to develop their own set of principles and become good citizens and humane adults. This is at the heart of what schools should be about. Not just the curriculum taught but the curriculum lived and modelled. This is ultimately down to the culture that leaders create in their schools and is influenced by their own behaviour as leaders. As Carolyn Roberts says at the end of her case study: 'Children deserve to see, every day, what it takes to live a good life, no matter what the weather brings.'

Summary

Authenticity
and Doing the
Right Thing

Those with an imperfect leadership mindset:

- Know that they make mistakes, and they are kind to themselves when they do, just as they are kind when their colleagues make mistakes.

- Know that authenticity is extremely important in leadership. Therefore, they don't try to be a perfect leader or necessarily to be the type of leader that external bodies may expect them to be. Instead, they are true to themselves – to their own values and personality.

- Try – day by day and month by month – to be a better version of themselves as a leader.

- Understand the importance of modelling the behaviours they want to see in their organisation.

- Look at ways in which the systems and processes in the organisation can be used to incentivise those kinds of behaviours.

- Take seriously the ethical issues and grey areas they find themselves dealing with, and flex their ethical muscles.

Exercises to try

- Use the VIA Character Strengths Survey to reflect on your strengths and look for ways you can use those strengths to help you become more authentically you.

▪ Describe to a friend, mentor or coach the leader you want to become. What do you want to be known for in terms of your values and ethical actions? Discuss what you might need to do to become more like that leader. Take time to revisit this and see how well you are doing at becoming your best authentic self.

Chapter 10
Showing Up with Hope and Pragmatism

The ultimate measure of a man is not where he stands in the moments of comfort and convenience, but where he stands at times of challenge and controversy.

Martin Luther King Jr

Imperfect leaders show up and walk into the wind. They are comfortable with what they can control and what they can't.

We have always known that controversy, crisis and uncertainty can make an appearance at any point in our leadership journey and present significant challenges to us and those we are leading. For example, at the time of writing, school leaders around the world continue to lead through the COVID-19 pandemic. Living through the pandemic is an experience that we all share. We know from the conversations that we have had with school leaders across the globe that the mindset and principles of imperfect leadership are highly relevant, and so it seems important to consider what we can learn about imperfect leadership when under significant strain. This chapter will refer back to many of the principles outlined in the first nine chapters of the book, but will consider how they apply in the most difficult of circumstances.

When the serious impact of the pandemic first struck in March 2020, schools in the UK, and in many other systems around the world, closed for the majority of their students, whilst staying open for the children of essential workers. School leaders had to write and implement new risk assessments and plans to minimise the obvious concerns for the staff and children who would remain in school, having to absorb and read at pace the rapidly changing government guidance. Teachers had to quickly adapt the way they worked to provide remote education for those students who were learning from home, as well as provide care and education for the children of essential workers in school. Leaders and IT technicians in our schools needed to provide extensive support to teachers to make this rapid change as many lacked confidence and experience in using some of the technology, as well as the skills in adapting to an online context.

Teachers and leaders had to consider and respond to the fact that many children and young people found themselves trying to work in the same room as their siblings, with neither the resources, the technical devices, the broadband access or the space to work effectively. For teachers, it was not as simple as just 'teaching online' in the same way you would teach in a classroom. The whole context had changed and we were all in unknown territory.

Most school leaders we know also recognised how important it was to reach out to their isolated communities and provide food hampers and support. In some cases, simply knocking on the door and waving through windows was a lifeline for some families – leaders and teachers who turned up on the doorstep to show a familiar face and to check that their vulnerable families were okay. And on top of this, for many school leaders and communities, there were and continue to be losses – friends and family members who didn't make it through. Leading school communities through grief and loss has been extraordinarily challenging for many.

The changes and the challenges for school leaders were unprecedented.

One entry on Twitter from a school leader in the middle of the pandemic read: 'My leadership development programme did not prepare me for this.' This school leader was right. No development programme can possibly prepare leaders to help them contend with the issues and challenges that they faced. They found themselves in uncharted territory. They were having to deal with issues that even the most experienced school leaders had never had to deal with before. There was no manual or mental map to fall back on.

Perhaps, what was most stressful was the need to make decisions about things that were outside their control or knowledge base. Many found themselves having to address health and welfare issues that could have life or death implications – a situation completely outside their professional experience. They found themselves soaking up the stress from anxious parents, worried colleagues and young people struggling with isolation, whilst also trying to cope with their own personal concerns about the health and well-being of their loved ones.

We have the deepest of respect for those who have been leading schools throughout the pandemic and the heroic and professional way they have helped to bring their schools, their students and their community through it.

Although there is no manual for leadership in a crisis, we do believe that there are some general principles of leadership that do apply in times of great uncertainty and that many of these have their roots in the principles of imperfect leadership.

Show up

The idea of 'showing up' during a crisis may seem very straightforward, but it is surprising the number of leaders who get this wrong.

In 2005, the south-eastern coast of the United States was devastated by Hurricane Katrina. More than 1,800 people lost their lives and there was at least US$160 billion in damage. Large parts of New Orleans had to be rebuilt. But President George Bush flew from his home in Texas over the devastation below and headed straight to the White House in Washington. There was an outcry at his apparent lack of concern for those who were struggling with the fallout of the hurricane, and some believe that his reputation as a leader never fully recovered.

In 1966, at Aberfan in Wales, a slag heap engulfed a school and killed 109 children and five teachers. The Queen felt she would be in the way – that she would be a distraction – and that others were more equipped to be there than her. It took eight days before she visited. According to royal sources, not going straight away to Aberfan after the disaster was one of the biggest regrets of her reign (Lees, 2002).

There are many more examples of leaders failing to show up when they really needed to be visible and present, and it is possible to understand why. Like the Queen, some leaders feel that they will get in the way and, moreover, there is a lot of strategic planning to do as well as many forms to fill in and emails to send. Better to leave it to others to be there.

However, it is essential that leaders show up, that they don't delegate – unless they are too ill to be there in person or it is physically impossible for them to be present. They may be tempted to step back to organise the strategic planning, confident that their team has it all under control. Of course, there will be a need for strategic planning and it may well be true that the team have it all under control, but that is not the point. In the middle of a crisis, especially in the early days, being present is crucial. The community and those they lead need their leader – the boss, the person ultimately in charge – to be there, to empathise, to connect, to show how important it is.

 ## Steve

When I was director of education, I received a telephone call from a secondary school principal. He said, 'I am calling you because I fear for my life.' He told me that he had made the decision to temporarily exclude a boy from the school and had brought his parents in to discuss it. But the father insisted that he could not and would not exclude his son. The principal then explained about the school's behaviour policy, the consequences and why his son was being excluded. 'You don't understand,' said the father. 'If you exclude my son then I will find you and hurt you – ask the police about me.' After he had left, the school principal spoke with a police constable who told him that the father was a gangster and a murderer and that the police could not protect him against such a violent man. That is when the school principal phoned me.

When I took the call, I had several options. I could have sent a school adviser into the school to help. I could have stayed in my office and called the police superintendent myself. But the first thing I did was to tell the principal that I would be there in fifteen minutes. I got in my car, drove to the school and made it clear that the principal would not be dealing with this on his own. I was going to stand alongside him, and my colleagues were going to manage it with him. In the end, we got some police protection and dealt with the exclusion hearing away from the school in the town hall. The problem went away. Years later, I bumped into the school principal at a concert, and he told me he would never forget what I had done for him at that time. When people are very stressed and extremely worried in a time of crisis, we show up.

Of course, during the height of the pandemic, during lockdowns, showing up wasn't as straightforward for leaders as it had been pre-pandemic. Because of the need to remain in 'bubbles' and mitigate against the spread of the virus, the ability to sit alongside staff in the staffroom at break or lunchtime or walk around classrooms at the start and end of the day, just to make connections and reassure the team, was harder. Never mind the fact that many members of the school team were now working from home, delivering teaching online.

However, we have been astounded by the number of leaders we know who found creative ways to show up despite these limitations. We know leaders who kept a Zoom call open all day, sharing the link with the whole staff team, so that they could just drop in and ask for help. We know leaders who got to school before anyone else just so they could leave notes, cards and chocolate bars in people's classrooms. Leaders who knew that being visible and connected was important, so sent personalised video or voice messages to staff, as well as running regular online staff briefings and meetings. Being an imperfect leader means that you find ways to show up, even when it is difficult and even though you may not have any immediate answers.

 ## Prompts for personal reflection

- Where, and for whom, do you need to show up more?

- What prevents you or holds you back from showing up in a crisis?

Walk into the wind

As imperfect leaders we don't just show up, we walk into the wind. Leadership can sometimes be extraordinarily hard and, for many, leading schools during the pandemic was definitely one of those times.

Walking into the wind is when leaders know that they need to do a really tough thing, their stomach is churning and they want to run away, but they actively choose to do that tough thing anyway. Walking into the wind is when leaders desperately want to turn over and stay under the duvet that morning because it is all so hard, but they get up and go into work and deal with that difficult issue. They know that if they make the easy choice and walk away from the problem, rather than the hard choice of dealing with the problem, then they will end up letting down their students and their school community. In times of uncertainty this can be immensely hard. Imperfect leaders know they don't have all the answers, but they do know that they need to be authentic and try to do the right thing.

The case study below from Susan Douglas illustrates this powerfully. As imperfect leaders we have to be prepared to 'be brave, walk into the wind and take control', particularly in a crisis where there is unlikely to be a rule book to follow. She describes how she was driven by her leadership instinct, but also critically the values of the organisation she leads.

 ## Case study

Susan Douglas, CEO, Eden Academy Trust, and senior schools adviser, British Council

The spring term of 2020 began like any other. At Eden we enjoyed our annual training day bringing together staff from across the trust, and at the British Council we welcomed ministers of education from over 100 countries to the Education World Forum. A day after this finished, Public Health England raised the risk level to the British public from the novel coronavirus, which had recently been detected in Wuhan, China, from 'very low' to 'low'. But, even by 11 March, when Eden held one of its regular board meetings, the sheer enormity of what was about to happen was still not apparent. Or at least, not to me; others were wiser. Sometime later, one of my trustees who lives in Italy shared the blog post she wrote about that meeting:

> I dialled in the day after our lockdown started and that's when I began to feel as if I was shouting and waving my arms from behind a pane of soundproofed, tinted glass. Somehow, the meeting agenda looked like a normal agenda. People asked me about the situation in Italy and cracked

a few jokes. We didn't talk about COVID-19 until we reached any other business. I cried afterwards out of frustration that we'd spent more time on GDPR [General Data Protection Regulation] than on what I was beginning to suspect might turn out to be a real-life disaster movie.

The situation evolved rapidly, and within a fortnight we waited for the prime minister to make the inevitable announcement that schools would close. But it was at this point that the pandemic threw up another surprise: while schools would close, students with EHCPs would need to continue to attend. As a trust of special schools, all of our students have EHCPs and, as such, life for us – the prime minister seemed to suggest – would carry on as normal.

The reasons for this decision were understandable given the vulnerability and needs of our students. But, at that point, our staff absence rates were already at critical levels and although we didn't have the capacity to test, I suspected many had the virus.

As the CEO of an organisation of over 700 employees I had a duty of care to staff members as well as our students. I had never faced a dilemma like this, and it had never felt so important. To be honest, I have hesitated to write this case study for fear of criticism or sanction, but our imperfect leadership could now be based only on instinct and the values upon which we had built our trust. As many have said, there simply wasn't a rule book for this.

What we knew and didn't know on 23 March 2020:

- Our students are among the most vulnerable in society and many are medically vulnerable. What we didn't know was how dangerous COVID-19 might be for them.

- Our students' disabilities mean they do not socially distance and most need hand-to-hand support to access education. Some use saliva as a sensory stimulant.

- Our staff have the same vulnerabilities as any other adults in relation to COVID-19, but the necessity of close contact in their roles meant they couldn't follow the same public health advice as the rest of society.

- Some of our families are isolated, both socially and geographically, and a national lockdown could potentially exacerbate this.

- Lots of our adults – both staff and families, in line with the rest of the population – were understandably frightened.

What we knew we had to do as leaders:

- **Be brave, walk into the wind and take control.** Despite guidance to the contrary, we initially closed our schools. We knew we needed time to regroup and to carefully think through new ways of working that would keep the staff and students as safe as possible. We also knew that many families wanted to keep their children at home, unclear at that point what the potential impact might be if they were to contract the virus. Putting significant effort and energy into creating remote learning and therapy services was essential.

- **Support each other.** One of the values of Eden Academies Trust is 'Together we are stronger', and this had never been more true. Twice-weekly heads of school meetings kept us all going, particularly after someone discovered the glory of Zoom backdrops which led to each meeting being 'themed' – on the beach, in space or maybe up a mountain. Always arranged so it was a surprise to me, it ensured that every meeting started with laughter. On the occasions when a head needed to turn their camera off during a meeting, we all knew what that meant. We kept Amazon drivers busy sending emergency welfare packages to try and wrap a virtual hug around whichever senior leader was finding things particularly tough.

- **Network with others and ask for help.** One of the tangible benefits of the pandemic is how much closer we now are to other schools, trusts and organisations. A wise friend pointed out that with the world in lockdown we were all equidistant from each other; I was as far from my neighbour as I was from my friend in Singapore. Colleagues were incredibly generous professionally with their time, advice and resources. I think we played our part too, and as we move forward, we will certainly continue to nurture the networks developed in times of crisis.

- **Gather round the family, not just the student.** Our families were potentially isolated, frightened and many more moved into difficult circumstances. Our family services team became the fourth emergency service for many of them. The signed 'recipe of the week' video, which went live on the website every Friday (with the associated ingredients dropped off on doorsteps early in the morning for those families that needed them), was a highlight.

- **Personalise our approach.** To staff as well as students. While national guidance was, of course, essential, we felt that it was important to empower our staff to contribute to their own risk assessments, allowing them to make a judgement about whether it was safe for them to come to school. This empathetic approach was well received, and we saw many examples of discretionary effort across the trust as a result.

So, did the pandemic change me as a leader? It certainly reminded me that there are times when being directive is essential, but as a leadership style the anxiety of this direction potentially being wrong was exhausting. It reinforced the importance of being empathetic and, critically, emphasised that being part of a professionally generous, collaborative network supports our ability to deliver optimistic and resilient leadership.

 ## Prompts for personal reflection

- When have you demonstrated leadership courage in the past and walked into the wind?

- What was it about that situation that enabled you to act in that way?

- How can you learn from this as you face new challenges?

Get comfortable with what you can control and what you cannot

Being an imperfect leader means that we know we cannot do everything, so we have a keen awareness of what is controllable and what is not controllable in the environment and context in which we are leading. This is particularly important when leading in a crisis or in times of great uncertainty.

We believe there are three factors that we can control as leaders during a crisis. Firstly, we are in control of our own personal leadership and the approach we take. Leading under pressure means adapting our personal leadership approach and becoming increasingly agile, visible, responsive, decisive, creative and flexible. In Chapter 1, we discussed at length the importance of adapting our leadership to match the context in which we find ourselves. Secondly, we have the ability to act – we are not totally powerless and cannot be dependent on someone else telling us what to do and when to do it. We don't evade our responsibility as leaders. We have to continue to lead, even in the absence of clarity from government or a policy to follow. Finally, we have knowledge – knowledge of the people we lead and the community we serve – but we also have the ability to learn more, to ask questions, to seek advice, to listen and to respond.

Of course, there are many things that are beyond our control, and for many leaders this is the biggest challenge. We want to fix things quickly, to make clear plans and provide answers and solutions for our schools. Imperfect leaders can acknowledge that some things are beyond our control and some things are unknown. But what is known is who we are as leaders and our ability to respond, based on our values and expertise.

Deal with the urgent but build in some space for the strategic and for the future

The urgent is essential – people need their leaders to help them address what is coming at them. Most school leaders will do this instinctively and rise to the challenges of the crisis. They may perhaps find themselves in more of a command-and-control role than they are used to, with their colleagues relying upon them for fast and timely decision-making. Sometimes, however, after a little while, leaders can find that the urgent becomes compelling and almost attractive. The adrenalin flows, leaders feel they are making a difference and responding to immediate needs. They sense the camaraderie with their team. Sometimes leaders can find the whole experience of leading in a crisis exhausting but surprisingly fulfilling. But even in a crisis, it is important not just to deal with the urgent but somehow to set some resource aside to look at the big picture.

In a blog post, Sir Michael Barber (2020) tells the story of how in 1940, London was at war, completely isolated and being bombed every night. An invasion of Britain was being planned by the Nazis, who had already overrun the rest of Western Europe. In that same year, a small number of senior officials from the then Board of Education settled into a few rooms at a hotel in Bournemouth and set about the task of designing a school system for after the war. Four years later, this provided the foundation for the 1944 Education Act and the post-war education system.

Even if leaders understand the importance of showing up, being visible and have their hands completely full in dealing with the urgency of the situation, they somehow need to find ways to step back and reflect upon the bigger, more strategic issues; to think about how they build for the future, not just how they respond to the present. This can be immensely hard to do and at times it might be necessary for some of the strategic planning to be delegated to others. The important thing is that the big picture and more long-term thinking is being done.

Times of crisis and uncertainty are usually horrible, but they also throw up new possibilities and opportunities. Clearly, COVID-19 has been a catastrophe. Millions of children globally are at risk of not returning to school after the pandemic. The temporary loss of other services that schools provide – in addition to teaching and learning – has had a big impact on the mental and physical health of millions of children around the world. There are increased concerns about mental ill health and safety of vulnerable children. However, the pandemic also presents school leaders with opportunities to think again about what they really want for their school rather than necessarily returning to the old normal.

During the lockdown, people really missed schools, not just for the chance for children to learn through a well-taught face-to-face curriculum but also for all the other hugely positive aspects of school life. We were reminded that for many young people, schools provide a feeling of safety and security that perhaps they don't get at home; a sense of order and expectations that may be lacking elsewhere. For some children, school may be the only place where they have a positive and valued relationship with a significant adult or the chance to spend time with a friend who likes and values them. Schools help us to explore possibilities – not just in classrooms with teachers but in all other kinds of social interactions that take place during the school day. They connect us with people who are not like us, as well as with those who are, encouraging us to embrace diversity and explore identity. During the lockdown, children missed going to school because they missed their friends, they missed the interaction, they missed that sense of belonging. The pandemic has helped to bring about a deeper public recognition about the purpose of schools and their place in our lives and a deeper respect for teachers.

In many cases, the pandemic has led to the building of stronger links between schools and parents and to a more effective and integrated use of technology. As a result, school leaders have come to value flexible working and virtual professional development in a way they might not have imagined before. It has also led to stronger collaboration between schools and other local services.

The lack of standardised tests and examinations in many systems during the pandemic has thrown up new thinking about the future of assessment and whether our existing accountability systems are fit for purpose.

For many leaders, the positive aspects that have arisen during the pandemic will be something they can build upon. There may be good opportunities to renew their commitment to their communities, to focus on more outward-facing collective responsibility rather than on top-down accountability, to explore how technology can be used in more effective ways to support teaching and learning, to review their approach to flexible working and job-sharing, and to further strengthen collaboration with other schools.

If school leaders are to ensure that they build something even better for their students and community as we come out of the pandemic, then they somehow need to find the opportunity to take a step back for some big-picture thinking.

Ask for help

We have dealt with this theme extensively in Chapter 3 – indeed, it is something that runs right through the book – but we believe that this is especially relevant in times of uncertainty. As Matt Hood outlines in his excellent case study below about the launch of Oak National Academy, in a crisis leaders cannot rely on developing expertise gradually. They need to ask for help from those who are already experts in their field.

 ## Case study

Matt Hood, founder and principal, Oak National Academy, England

When the Chinese government announced it had 'locked down' Wuhan, a city of 11 million people, in January 2020 the very idea of a lockdown seemed preposterous.

But it was China. Authoritarian regimes can do things that western democracies cannot. Or so I thought. Within weeks, the UK was locked down too. Schools were largely closed and teachers and parents were grappling with the challenges of home education for 8.5 million students.

A year on, and the team at Oak National Academy and its wider partnership had delivered over 130 million lessons to millions of students from around the world. Our platform is zero rated (which means families don't pay for data to use it), accessible and bulletproof when it comes to handling traffic (we had around 2.5 million students per week in January 2020). Whilst any curriculum, unit or lesson can always be better, our broad curriculum of over twenty subjects (including curricula for the specialist sector) is built on rigorous foundations and empirical evidence about how learning works.

We had done all of this without ever actually meeting each other. In the middle of a global pandemic. For the cost of one average sized secondary school.

How? A big part of Oak's success comes down to context. That isn't to take away from the extraordinary efforts of our team and wider partnership. It is simply to acknowledge that we started up in a national crisis when people were unusually willing to act quickly and trust each other. But, whilst important, timing doesn't explain it all.

Team of experts

The first thing we had was a team of experts. Things started organically. During the Easter holiday, a question here turned into a WhatsApp message there. A simple exam question formed. Within a week, could an interdisciplinary team of volunteers make a contribution to the national effort by creating a national online school, free for everyone?

We had our first team meeting on Good Friday. By this point, we were a team of six with a range of expertise from different disciplines. We launched Oak National Academy with our first week of lessons, 180 in total, nine days later.

Why does expertise matter? Expertise allows people to efficiently and effectively solve the persistent problems they face in their day-to-day roles. These problems are solved using sophisticated mental models (a fancy term for what someone knows and how that knowledge is organised). These mental models (their expertise) are built over the years by acquiring new knowledge and applying it consistently.

This expertise doesn't easily transfer: change the role someone is responsible for and you change the persistent problems they have to solve. The bigger the change in role, the bigger the difference in the problems. And the more different the persistent problems are, the less efficiently and effectively an individual is at solving them. In effect, the less expert the person becomes.

Understanding this is critical when it comes to building teams. If Oak was going to work, each of the spots in my top team needed to be filled by someone who was unusually good at solving the persistent problems that were going to come with that role. And not only did individuals need to know their stuff. Their colleagues needed them to know it too, so that we could build trust at breakneck pace and get the finished product over the line.

In a crisis, or indeed anytime when important work is done, it is domain-specific expertise that matters. If you have time on your side individuals can develop the expertise they might need for a role, but in a crisis there is no time for that. Problem-solving started in our first meeting.

Generous relationships

Oak exists because we were able to swiftly draw on a range of relationships and convince others to take this leap with us. Schools and school trusts gave us their curriculum and teachers. Communications agencies created our brand and launch plan. Technology companies gave us free access to platforms and hosting. Education charities seconded their staff. The Department for Education provided us with an emergency COVID grant.

As I said at the start, some of this was down to timing – people were unusually willing to help. But it also came down to our network. Networking has a bad reputation. I understand why. Nobody wants to be described as 'a bit of a networker'. Is there anything more awkward than those drinks events when you show up alone, take a warm glass of wine you don't want and attempt to 'work the room'?

It is not this type of networking I am advocating. It is a more genuine type of relationship-building through helping others that was drummed into me as a kid. First by the Methodist Church who taught me to 'do all the good you can', second by my school where the motto was 'lead in order to serve' and third by the Scouts who always reminded me that 'you get out what you put in'.

Put simply, I was taught to show up and help out – without expectation of a return. Years of doing this across my team meant that when it mattered, when the Bat-Signal went up, folks came to help – also without any expectation of a return. We would be nowhere if they hadn't.

Deliberate culture

Pulling a week of lessons out of the bag was just the start. We had to repeat this process every week for ten weeks. Then create 10,000 lessons in one go in preparation for September. And then have them all zero rated so there were no data charges.

None of this would have been possible without a focus on our culture. There would be no Oak without our team. And teams stick around in conditions where they can focus on doing their very best work.

I come from the Patty McCord school when it comes to a culture that creates these conditions (McCord, 2018). I value three things – or, put another way, I have three values:

1. **Freedom.** The organisation needs to give people the freedom to make decisions without a huge bureaucratic machine getting in their way. Individuals need to take that freedom, step up and use it.

2. **Responsibility.** The flip side of freedom is responsibility. The organisation needs to communicate clear, simple, shared objectives. People need to think about these shared objectives, not just their own objectives, when making decisions.

3. **Continuous improvement.** The organisation needs to provide every opportunity to help develop the expertise of its team, including creating regular opportunities for radically candid feedback (Scott, 2017). Individuals need to prioritise these opportunities in their work.

At Oak, these values don't get put up on the wall (we don't have any walls!). We also have lots more work to do here. But I try to keep them front of mind when making practical day-to-day decisions.

So, whilst the moment created by the pandemic mattered, it was a team of experts, their generous relationships and a deliberate culture that was able to take advantage of that moment and create something special that we hope made a small contribution to a national effort over a difficult period.

School leaders are often put on the spot when there is an emergency or crisis. Parents and staff expect them to be able to answer their queries and respond to their concerns. Leaders do need to know enough to be able to do that and to be able to provide reassurance and understanding. But they also need to refer to experts and get support when the boundaries of their knowledge and expertise are reached. Nobody has all the answers. The more leaders can talk things through with others in similar situations and tap into the expertise of those with more knowledge of the issues, the better.

 ## Marie-Claire

In March 2020, very early on in the pandemic, the KYRA partnership of schools in Lincolnshire set up a WhatsApp group to increase connection and communication at a time when it was easy to feel alone or isolated. It was humorously called KYRA COBRA – our local response to matters of national emergency, mirroring the UK government committee.

With over seventy members, this community of school leaders created a culture and openness to ask for help, share resources, get a second opinion, let off steam and support one another through our darkest days as school leaders. Watching how this group of leaders cared for one another during the pandemic has been utterly inspirational.

One leader would say, 'I'm struggling with X or Y' or 'I'm on my knees,' and another would step in and say, 'I'll give you a ring' or 'Can I help?' Every time there was a new government announcement or change, this group would respond, sharing our understanding and discussing how we were going to respond in our context. Several times, school leaders would reach out to say that they themselves were now ill or self-isolating, and other leaders in the community would volunteer to step in to support the deputy head teacher or assistant head teacher who were being thrown into 'acting headship' in the midst of a pandemic. In at least two cases, KYRA leaders voluntarily took on acting headship of one another's schools, working with other local governing bodies to ensure our schools could continue to operate.

No one compelled these schools to work like this. It came from a deeply engrained sense that we would be better together, and that no school leader should be on their own grappling with the pandemic in isolation.

At the time of writing, when we are still not meeting face to face, this group continues to thrive, with a document bank full of shared resources, regular Zoom calls and a culture where asking for help is the norm. This is the KYRA mantra in action: 'Give what you can, ask for what you need and pay it forward'.

Lead with pragmatic optimism

Optimism is important, but blind optimism is dangerous. In the course of managing the pandemic, it would have been foolish for leaders to respond by assuring everyone that everything was going to be okay, that no one would get ill and that it would be over soon. There are dangers in overpromising and then under-delivering. That leads to distrust and despair. What we need is pragmatic optimism.

Many readers will know the story in Jim Collins' book *Good to Great* (2001, pp. 83–85) about the Stockdale Paradox. Admiral Jim Stockdale was the highest-ranking United States military officer in the 'Hanoi Hilton' prisoner-of-war camp during the height of the Vietnam War. Tortured over twenty times during his eight-year imprisonment from 1965 to 1973, he lived out the war without any certainty as to whether he would survive to see his family again. He was asked later why he survived when so many others did not. He said that the optimists never made it out. The optimists, he said, kept thinking they would be 'out by Christmas' or 'out by Easter' and they couldn't cope with the disappointment when these dates passed by without being released. Stockdale said he found a way to stay alive by embracing the harshness of his situation but doing so with a balance of healthy optimism. He described it as a paradox: 'You must never confuse faith that you will prevail in the end – which you can never afford to lose – with the discipline to confront the most brutal facts of your current reality, whatever they might be' (Collins, 2001, p. 85).

This is relevant to how school leaders need to lead during times of crisis and uncertainty. Optimism is a fundamentally good attitude to have – to be positive when those around us are doubting and troubled. But, on its own, optimism is not sufficient. We also need to confront the brutal facts. We need to be honest and face the reality of what we are dealing with. We also need to accept the situation for what it is.

Part of our role as leaders is to prepare people for tough times; to be frank about bad news and about the challenges ahead. In doing so, we need to put ourselves fully in the shoes of those we are leading. What they need from us is honesty, clarity and empathy. We have witnessed some leaders making the mistake of overemphasising the tough times and problems they themselves face as leaders – as if it is all about *them* and what a hard time *they* are having! No wonder their staff feel ground down and unhappy. We have also seen others be over-optimistic, hoping that the worst won't happen and therefore avoiding thinking about the challenges they might encounter. As imperfect leaders we do need to confront reality. We hope for the best, whilst planning and preparing for the worst. In the midst of these challenging times, we need to be pragmatic and realistic but cheerfulness is also an essential element. Our colleagues need it from us.

 ## Steve

When I was 15 – a year before the crucial external O level examinations – I was fifth bottom of the bottom set in French. Before he died, my dad gave me copies of my old school reports and I was particularly interested to look up what my French report said for that year. My French teacher had only written one word: 'Cheerful'. When you are fifth bottom of the bottom set a year before your O levels, being cheerful – on its own – is not enough. You have got to work harder and improve and deliver. You must be pragmatic. Being cheerful is a good thing, but I also needed to confront the brutal facts and take some realistic, concerted action. I actually did that and scraped my O level French.

Lead with hope

Readers will be familiar with the term 'learned helplessness', which relates to how people can, over time, feel increasingly disempowered and become dependent on others. It is easy for this to happen in times of crisis and uncertainty; leaders feel unable to control things and gradually they become despondent, adopting a victim mindset.

In contrast, we love Michael Fullan's (2021, p. 39) concept of 'learned hopefulness'. Results of many studies show that hope is a significant factor in supporting positive mental health and well-being, and the good news is that hopefulness can be cultivated.

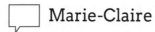 ## Marie-Claire

During times of high stress and pressure, and when leading in a crisis, I have found a few ways to help me stay hopeful. Firstly, taking time to acknowledge the things that I can control and the things I cannot – and using that exercise to develop a sense of agency about my own leadership. Secondly, setting goals for myself, even small daily goals, to help me see what I am achieving, even under extremely difficult circumstances. Thirdly, reminding myself that challenges and obstacles are inevitable and that there will be multiple ways of overcoming each challenge. This helps me to stay flexible and agile and not get too stuck in one particular solution. The path to my goal might not be the easiest, most straightforward or shortest route, but it is still possible to make progress towards that goal. Finally, practising gratitude and self-compassion has been profoundly helpful.

Being able to acknowledge the pain and difficulties we face as leaders, whilst simultaneously being future orientated and upbeat, is a powerful (if paradoxical) mental mindset to develop. It is important for leaders to seek out positive opportunities and try to find ways to achieve some quick wins. This can lead to a more optimistic culture and a sense of hope that things can be better. Gradually, this can become engrained in the culture.

 ## Prompts for personal reflection

Practise professional self-care. Ask yourself these questions:

- What do you value most about the job you do?

- What are (or do you expect to be) the most stressful and the most rewarding aspects of leading through a crisis?

- How do you know when you are stressed?

- How might your co-workers know when you are stressed?

- What can others do for you when you are stressed?

- What can you do for yourself?

Be a storyteller

Stories have always been important to humans. Whether it is paintings on an ancient cave wall or the lyrics of a song passed down from generation to generation, telling the story of our collective experience and history is part of our shared humanity.

 Steve

Many years ago, I visited a secondary school in the south of England. The building was pretty run-down to be honest, but the head teacher was so optimistic. She said, 'I know the building isn't up to much, but the staff are fantastic – we think of it as like Lewis Hamilton driving a Ford Fiesta.' Later, when I talked to her leadership team, they described her as their storyteller. They told me that when things are very challenging – and they often are in the school – she tells them the story of how they are going to move forward and how it will get better. I like the idea of the leader as storyteller, as the one who elicits hope and provides encouragement and positivity.

However, imperfect leaders know that telling the story – putting words to experience and creating a narrative to describe the journey – is not something you do in retrospect.

Imperfect leaders use stories to give hope, to frame the future and to acknowledge the present and the past. We need stories to inspire us for, and on, our journey.

 ## Marie-Claire

As the leader of a group of schools, I was extremely aware of the need to help our school leaders describe what they were feeling at various points during the pandemic, to frame their experiences and normalise them. I did a lot of research and reading and found various models which seemed helpful. One example is below. This was adapted to help us talk about our collective experience of the pandemic.

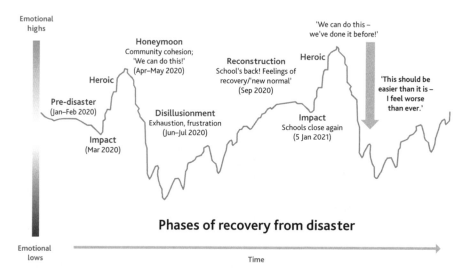

Phases of recovery from disaster (adapted from Zunin and Myers, as cited in DeWolfe, 2000, p. 5)

The well-known English author Philip Pullman puts it like this: 'We need a story, a myth that does what the traditional religious stories did. It must explain. It must satisfy our hunger for a why ... and there are two kinds of why. And our story must deal with both. There is the one that asks what brought us here? And the other that asks what are we here for?' (quoted in Gilbert, 2007, p. 22).

In times of crisis, we need to find ways to tell the story of how we are all going to get through and out the other side, what brought us here and what we are here for. We need to develop a compelling narrative for the future whilst reminding those we lead of our mission in the first place. We help people to see what the future can be like – something that excites and enthuses our colleagues. But we also need to plan rigorously – and in uncertain times that might need to include plans B and C as well as plan A – to manage risk, to stay focused on what really matters and to know where we are on the journey.

It is also important to remember to retell the story and adapt the narrative as time moves on and we come out of times of crisis and uncertainty. As leaders we need to use our storytelling to meet people where they are at and move them together towards our shared vision for the future.

 Prompt for personal reflection

- When the pressure is on, and you are leading in a time of crisis or uncertainty, it can be harder to recall and recapture the narrative for those you lead. With the nuance and sensitivity required, how can you remind people of why their work and their role is so important? Can you describe what is still going well, despite the challenges?

Summary

Showing Up with Hope
and Pragmatism

None of us were taught how to lead in a pandemic and it isn't on any leadership development programme, but what we can do as imperfect leaders is:

- Understand the importance of showing up in a crisis, even if we don't know all the answers.

- Choose to walk into the wind because we know it is the right thing to do.

- Focus on things that are within our control.

- Find a way of focusing on the strategic as well as the urgent and operational.

- Seek out expertise from others rather than pretending that we know the answers.

- Show optimism combined with pragmatism and let cheerfulness break through.

Exercises to try

- Take a piece of A4 paper and divide it into three columns.

- In the first column, make a list of all the concerns you have which you know you have no influence or control over. During the pandemic there have been so many issues that school leaders have no ability to influence or control. This has led to high levels of stress in the profession. Just noting these down and being consciously aware of that challenge can be a helpful activity to settle the mind. When we are leading in a crisis there are many things over which we have no control.

- In the second column, list the concerns that you have that you know you can influence. For example, we can influence our colleagues (but we cannot control them!) and we can influence the culture and atmosphere in our schools.

- Finally, note in the final column the things that you can control. Problems we have control over often involve our own behaviour, actions and attitudes, as well as how we deploy people in our organisations, and what we prioritise.

Concern	Influence	Control
Things I have no influence on and cannot control	Things I can influence	Things I can control

(adapted from Covey, 2020)

By doing this exercise we can determine where we are focusing most of our time and energy, and use it to reflect on how proactive and responsive we are being. For example:

- *Reactive* people often get fixated on concerns over which they cannot exert influence or control. Often, leaders who think they are perfect find themselves operating here. They focus on the weaknesses of other people, the limitations they feel they have to lead under, and circumstances over which they have no control. This can often lead to blaming and accusing attitudes, as well as reactive negative language. This fixation means that leaders' energy isn't directed towards the things that they could in fact influence.

- *Proactive* people focus their efforts on the things they can influence. They work on the things they can do something about. Stephen Covey (2020) asserts that by diverting your attention to those items and issues you can influence, you indirectly affect the items and issues of concern.

In times of uncertainty and crisis, the main thing to concentrate on and be especially attentive to is the quality of your own thinking and your response to the stress and pressure. Prioritising your own well-being (including how you rest and recover) is vital. This will help you to show up and be the imperfect (but present) leader that your team and community need you to be.

Chapter 11
The Imperfect Leadership Mindset

We believe that by adopting an imperfect leadership mindset, we open the door to growth, development and learning for ourselves and for the organisations we lead. By acknowledging that we are leaders who don't know it all, we use our limitations and imperfections as a motivation to keep learning and growing.

Throughout this book, we have tried to guide the reader through a number of different themes, with illustrations, case studies, reflections and exercises to try. However, a note of caution: the imperfect leadership mindset is not a pick-and-mix! Each one of these chapters contains elements of the imperfect leadership mindset which we recommend you explore and adopt. It is also important to note that there are multiple synergies between the chapters, with some overarching themes and connections. For example, by asking for help you could simultaneously be developing and empowering your teams.

We have included a summary of the following key messages:

① Self-Awareness and Tuning into Context	Imperfect leaders are self-aware. They know their strengths, but they are also aware of their weaknesses. They tune into their context and adapt their leadership accordingly.
② Developing and Empowering Teams	Imperfect leaders develop and empower their team without losing sight of the impact on the front line.
③ Asking for Help	Imperfect leaders are invitational in their approach. They ask for help and are not afraid to admit that they need it. They create a help-seeking culture.
④ Managing Ego and Acknowledging Mistakes	Imperfect leaders cultivate a healthy ego, and this means they can admit their mistakes and put things right.
⑤ Making Public Promises	Imperfect leaders know how and when to make public promises, and they elicit commitment from others.

6 Being a Restless Learner	Imperfect leaders are curious about themselves and understand that they are never the finished product. They are also deeply curious about others.
7 Power and Love	Imperfect leaders show power in their leadership, but they also show love.
8 Developing Future Leaders	Imperfect leaders encourage others to step up to leadership.
9 Authenticity and Doing the Right Thing	Imperfect leaders know themselves and are authentic. They show others the best version of themselves. Imperfect leaders try to do the right thing.
10 Showing Up with Hope and Pragmatism	Imperfect leaders show up and walk into the wind. They are comfortable with what they can control and what they can't. They are the chief storyteller and lead with pragmatic optimism and with hope.

Final Thoughts

When we were young, most of us looked up to head teachers, principals and other public service leaders as significant figures and worthy of our respect. Then we made our way in our career in education and, at some point, we looked round and realised that it is our generation that is now occupying those same roles. We became the people in charge. We hoped for great leaders to come along and help to build a sustainable future for our world, and then it dawned on us that, as leaders in education, we are the ones who are now entrusted with that role. To quote Alice Walker (2006): 'We are the ones we have been waiting for'. This happens to every generation and it can be a daunting realisation.

It is happening now to those school leaders who find themselves leading during the pandemic and beyond. As senior school leaders, the children and young people, the parents, the local community and all the staff are relying on you to lead them and to do well for them. The sense of responsibility can be overpowering if you dwell on it. But it will be made even more daunting if you have a view of leadership as some kind of transformational, individualistic, super-hero model that most of us can never aspire to be. That will just make you feel inadequate.

Once people adopt an imperfect leadership mindset it doesn't sort out all their problems, but it does stop them from trying to pretend that they are someone they are not, and it does help them to feel less isolated. Rather than pretending they can do it all themselves, leaders who know they don't know it all seek out help and surround themselves with people – internally and externally – who can play a part in this great endeavour. Because they are honest and act with integrity, and because they keep their promises and aim to show love as well as power in their leadership, people warm to them and want them to be successful.

Moreover, those with an imperfect leadership mindset don't take all the glory for themselves; instead, they acknowledge the contribution of others, which makes people even more keen to help them. They show up in a crisis, even when their stomach is churning, not because they think they know all the answers but because they know it is the right thing to do. They are willing to take on new challenges because they know that nobody is the finished product and that the best leaders are restless learners. And when they do make mistakes, they may (for a while) give themselves a hard time, but they understand that everyone makes mistakes, so they are kind to themselves and then move on to the next challenge. Their aim is not to be perfect but to be a better version of themselves tomorrow.

The great thing is that imperfect leadership is neither a set of competencies to be mastered nor a body of knowledge to be memorised. It is a mindset to be embraced. And adopting that mindset won't necessarily make your leadership less challenging, but it should help to make it feel less lonely.

Both of us have found leadership in education to be one of the most challenging, tiring, exciting, joyous and deeply fulfilling things we could have possibly done with our lives. Our deep hope is that those in leadership roles who are reading this book will have been re-energised and reassured by the concept of imperfect leadership and that those who are considering stepping into a leadership role will be even more encouraged to do so.

As you lead your school community into the future you may be worried about the challenges ahead, but you have got this and you can do it.

In his poem 'Looking for the Castle, Second Time Around', William Ayot (2012) says that it is time to put away our self-doubt as leaders and step forward along the path:

> It is time to stop looking upwards at others
>
> What you have is enough
>
> What you are is ready.[1]

---

1   From 'Looking for the Castle, Second Time Around' by William Ayot: From *E-Mail from the Soul: New & Selected Leadership Poems*. Glastonbury: PS Avalon. Used with permission from the author.

Bibliography

Abraham, M. (2020) 'From founding documents to guiding frameworks: innovation at HPSS (Part 2)', *Principal Possum* (31 January). Available at: http://principalpossum.blogspot.com/2020/01/from-founding-documents-to-guiding_31.html.

Allen, B. (2019) 'Improving teachers' instructional practice: critically important, but incredibly hard to do', in C. Scutt and S. Harrison (eds), *Teacher CPD: International Trends, Opportunities and Challenges*. London: Chartered College of Teaching, pp. 112–117. Available at: https://my.chartered.college/wp-content/uploads/2019/11/Chartered-College-International-Teacher-CPD-report.pdf.

Atkin, J. (1996) 'From values and beliefs about learning to principles and practice'. Available at: https://www.education.sa.gov.au/sites/default/files/from_values_and_beliefs_about_learning_to_principles_and_practice.pdf.

Avolio, B. J., Luthans, F. and Walumbwa, F. O. (2004) 'Authentic leadership: theory building for veritable sustained performance'. Working paper. Lincoln, NE: Gallup Leadership Institute, University of Nebraska–Lincoln.

Ayot, W. (2012) *E-Mail from the Soul: New & Selected Leadership Poems*. Glastonbury: PS Avalon.

Barber, M. (2020) 'Finding time to build a better future: a note to leaders of schools and other places of learning', *Big Education* (30 April). Available at: https://bigeducation.org/learning-from-lockdown/lfl-content/finding-time-to-build-a-better-future.

Basford, T. E., Offermann, L. R. and Behrend, T. S. (2014) 'Please accept my sincerest apologies: examining follower reactions to leader apology', *Journal of Business Ethics*, 119(1), 99–117.

Baumeister, R. F. (2019) 'Stalking the true self through the jungles of authenticity: problems, contradictions, inconsistencies, disturbing findings – and a possible way forward', *Review of General Psychology*, 23(1), 143–154.

Bever, L. (2019) 'Doctor who was dragged, screaming, from United Airlines flight finally breaks silence', *Washington Post* (9 April). Available at: https://www.washingtonpost.com/transportation/2019/04/09/doctor-who-was-dragged-screaming-united-airlines-flight-finally-breaks-silence.

Bishop, R. (2019) *Teaching to the North-East: Relationship-Based Learning in Practice*. Wellington: NZCER Press.

Bresman, H. and Rao, V. D. (2017) 'A survey of 19 countries shows how Generations X, Y, and Z are – and aren't – different', *Harvard Business Review* (25 August). Available at: https://hbr.org/2017/08/a-survey-of-19-countries-shows-how-generations-x-y-and-z-are-and-arent-different.

Brown, B. (2010) 'The power of vulnerability' [video], *TED.com* (June). Available at: https://www.ted.com/talks/brene_brown_the_power_of_vulnerability?language=en.

Brown, B. (2018) *Dare to Lead: Brave Work. Tough Conversations. Whole Hearts*. New York: Random House.

Brown, B. (2020) 'Leadership, family and service' [podcast interview with Barack Obama]. Available at: https://brenebrown.com/transcript/brene-with-president-barack-obama-on-leadership-family-and-service.

Bryk, A. S. and Schneider, B. (2003) 'Trust in schools: a core resource for school reform', *Educational Leadership*, 60(6), 40–45.

Buckingham, M. and Clifton, D. O. (2001) *Now, Discover Your Strengths*. New York: Free Press.

Collins, J. (2001) *Good to Great: Why Some Companies Make the Leap … and Others Don't*. New York: Random House.

Collins, J. (2017) 'Getting the right people in the right seats over time'. Available at: https://www.jimcollins.com/media_topics/inTheRightSeats.html.

Committee on Standards in Public Life (1995) 'The seven principles of public life' (31 May). Available at: https://www.gov.uk/government/publications/the-7-principles-of-public-life.

Costin, C. (2014) 'Implementing system-wide change (fast) in education: the case of Rio de Janeiro'. Presentation for the World Bank, Washington, DC, 18 February. Available at: https://www.worldbank.org/en/events/2014/02/13/education-rio-de-janeiro.

Covey, S. R. (2020) *The 7 Habits of Highly Effective People: Powerful Lessons in Personal Change*, rev. edn. New York: Simon & Schuster.

Covey, S. R. and Merrill, R. R. (2006) *The Speed of Trust: The One Thing That Changes Everything*. New York: Free Press.

DeWolfe, D. J. (2000) *Training Manual for Mental Health and Human Service Workers in Major Disasters*, 2nd edn. Washington, DC: US Department of Health and Human Services, Substance Abuse and Mental Health Services Administration, Center for Mental Health Services.

Donaldson, D. (2010) *Teaching Scotland's Future: Report of a Review of Teacher Education in Scotland*. Edinburgh: Scottish Government.

Donohoo, J., Hattie, J. and Eells, R. (2018) 'The power of collective efficacy', *Educational Leadership*, 75(6), 40–44.

Dowd, M. (2018) 'Lady of the Rings: Jacinda Rules', *The New York Times* (September 8). Available at: https://www.nytimes.com/2018/09/08/opinion/sunday/jacinda-ardern-new-zealand-prime-minister.html.

Dubreuil, P., Forest, J., Gillet, N., Fernet, C., Landry, A., Crevier-Braud, L. and Girouard, S. (2016) 'Facilitating well-being and performance through the development of strengths at work: results from an intervention program', *International Journal of Applied Positive Psychology*, 1(1–3), 1–19.

Dudley, P. (2014) *Lesson Study: A Handbook*. Available at: https://lessonstudy.co.uk/lesson-study-a-handbook.

Dweck, C. S. (2006) *Mindset: The New Psychology of Success*. New York: Random House.

Ecclestone, K. (2011) 'Emotionally-vulnerable subjects and new inequalities: the educational implications of an "epistemology of the emotions"', *International Studies in Sociology of Education*, 21(2), 91–113, DOI: 10.1080/09620214.2011.575100

Edmondson, A. C. (2002) 'Managing the risk of learning: psychological safety in work teams'. Harvard Business School Working Paper, No. 02-062 (March). Available at: https://www.hbs.edu/faculty/Pages/item.aspx?num=12333.

Edmondson, A. C. (2019) *The Fearless Organization: Creating Psychological Safety in the Workplace for Learning, Innovation, and Growth*. Hoboken, NJ: John Wiley & Sons.

References

Elwick, A. and McAleavy, T. (2015) *Interesting Cities: Five Approaches to Urban School Reform*. Reading: Education Development Trust.

Ericsson, K. A., Krampe, R. T. and Tesch-Römer, C. (1993) 'The role of deliberate practice in the acquisition of expert performance', *Psychological Review*, 100(3), 363–406.

Ezard, T. (2021) *Ferocious Warmth: School Leaders Who Inspire and Transform*. N.p.: Tracey Ezard Pty.

Foa, R. S., Klassen, A., Slade, M., Rand, A. and R. Collins (2020) *The Global Satisfaction with Democracy Report 2020*. Cambridge: Centre for the Future of Democracy. Available at: https://www.bennettinstitute. cam.ac.uk/publications/global-satisfaction-democracy-report-2020.

Fromm, J. (2018) 'Gen Z in the workforce: how to recruit and retain youth generations', *Forbes* (3 July). Available at: https://www.forbes.com/sites/jefffromm/2018/07/03/gen-z-in-the-work-force-how-to-recruit-and-retain-youth-generations.

Fullan, M. (2018) *Nuance: Why Some Leaders Succeed and Others Fail*. Thousand Oaks, CA: Corwin Press.

Fullan, M. (2021) *The right drivers for whole system success*. Victoria, Australia: Centre for Strategic Education.

Gilbert, C. (2017) *Optimism of the Will: The Development of Local Area-Based Education Partnerships. A Think-Piece*. London: Centre for Leadership in Learning, UCL Institute of Education.

Gilbert, P. (2007) 'The spiritual foundation: awareness and context for people's lives today', in M. E. Coyte, P. Gilbert and V. Nicholls (eds), *Spirituality, Values and Mental Health: Jewels for the Journey*. London and Philadelphia, PA: Jessica Kingsley, pp. 19–43.

Goffee, R. and Jones, G. (2016) *Why Should Anyone Be Led By You? What It Takes to Be an Authentic Leader*. Boston, MA: Harvard Business Review Press.

Goleman, D. (2000) 'Leadership that gets results', *Harvard Business Review* (March/April). Available at: https://hbr.org/2000/03/leadership-that-gets-results.

Greany, T. (2018) *Sustainable Improvement in Multi-School Groups: Research Report*. London: Department for Education. Available at: https://www.gov.uk/government/publications/sustainable-improvement-in-multi-school-groups.

Grissom, J., Egalite, A. and Lindsay, C. (2021) *How Principals Affect Students and Schools: A Systematic Synthesis of Two Decades of Research*. New York: Wallace Foundation. Available at: http://www. wallacefoundation.org/principalsynthesis.

Hanifan, L. J. (1916) 'The rural school community center', *Annals of the American Academy of Political and Social Science*, 67(1), 130–138.

Hargreaves, D. H. (2001) 'A capital theory of school effectiveness and improvement', *British Educational Research Journal*, 27(4), 487–503.

Hargreaves, D. H. (2010) *Creating a Self-Improving School System*. Nottingham: National College for Teaching and Leadership. Available at: https://www.gov.uk/government/publications/creating-a-self-improving-school-system.

Hargreaves, D. H. (2012) *A Self-Improving School System: Towards Maturity*. Nottingham: National College for Teaching and Leadership. Available at: https://www.gov.uk/government/publications/a-self-improving-school-system-towards-maturity.

Hetrick, A. L., Blocker, L. D., Fairchild, J. and Hunter, S. T. (2021) 'To apologize or justify: leader responses to task and relational mistakes', *Basic and Applied Social Psychology*, 43(1), 30–45.

James, H. (ed.) (1920) *The Letters of William James, Vol. I.* Boston, MA: Little, Brown.

Kahane, A. (2010) *Power and Love: A Theory and Practice of Social Change.* San Francisco, CA: Berrett-Koehler.

Kaufman, S. B. (2019) 'Authenticity under fire', *Scientific American* (14 June). Available at: https://blogs. scientificamerican.com/beautiful-minds/authenticity-under-fire.

King Jr, M. L. (1963) *Strength to Love.* New York: Harper & Row.

Knox, R. E. and Inkster, J. A. (1968) 'Postdecision dissonance at post time', *Journal of Personality and Social Psychology*, 8(4, Pt 1), 319–323.

Lakey, C., Kernis, M., Heppner, W. and Lance, C. (2008) 'Individual differences in authenticity and mindfulness as predictors of verbal defensiveness', *Journal of Research in Personality*, 42(1), 230–238.

Lees, R. (2002) 'Aberfan: Queen's "biggest regret"', *South Wales Echo* (21 January).

Le Menestrel, M. (2011) Values, Ethics and Business Decisions. The Individual, Business and Corruption: The Changmaï Case. International MBA, Renmin University of China, Beijing. Available at: https://marc-lemenestrel.net/IMG/pdf/corruption.pdf.

Lencioni, P. M. (2002) *The Five Dysfunctions of a Team: A Leadership Fable.* San Francisco, CA: Jossey-Bass.

Lester, T. (2012) *Da Vinci's Ghost: Genius, Obsession, and How Leonardo Created the World in His Own Image.* New York: Free Press.

Linley, P. (2008) *Average to A +: Realising Strengths in Yourself and Others.* Coventry: CAPP Press.

Logue, C. (1969) *Selected Poems.* London: Faber & Faber.

Lucas, B., Claxton, G. and Spencer, E. (2013) 'Progression in student creativity in school: first steps towards new forms of formative assessments'. OECD Education Working Paper No. 86. Available at: https://www. oecd.org/education/ceri/5k4dp59msdwk.pdf.

Luft, J. and Ingham, H. (1955) 'The Johari window: a graphic model for interpersonal relations', in *Proceedings of the Western Training Laboratory in Group Development.* Los Angeles, CA: University of California, Los Angeles.

McCord, P. (2018) *Powerful: Building a Culture of Freedom and Responsibility.* San Francisco, CA: Silicon Guild.

Miglianico, M., Dubreuil, P., Miquelon, P., Bakker, A. B. and Martin-Krumm, C. (2020) 'Strength use in the workplace: a literature review', *Journal of Happiness Studies*, 21(2), 737–764. Available at: https://hal. univ-lorraine.fr/hal-02932138/document.

Munby, S. (2019) *Imperfect Leadership: A Book for Leaders Who Know They Don't Know It All.* Carmarthen: Crown House Publishing.

Munby, S. (2020a) *A New Paradigm for Leadership Development.* Occasional Paper No. 164. Melbourne: Centre for Strategic Education. Available at: https://atrico.org/wp-content/uploads/2020/05/Occasional-Paper-164-February-2020.pdf.

Munby, S. (2020b) 'The development of school leadership practices for 21st century schools', *European Journal of Education, Research, Development and Policy*, 55(2), 146–150. Available at: https://atrico.org/ wp-content/uploads/2019/11/The-development-of-school-leadership-practices-for-21st-century-schools.pdf.

Munby, S. and Fullan, M. (2016) *Inside-Out and Downside-Up: How Leading from the Middle Has the Power to Transform Education Systems. A Think/Action Piece*. Reading: Education Development Trust. Available at: https://michaelfullan.ca/wp-content/uploads/2016/02/Global-Dialogue-Thinkpiece.pdf.

Murphy, D. (2020) 'What Improv, Ubuntu, and Covid-19 have taught me about leadership'. Presidential address to the British Psychological Society Conference [online], September. Available at: https://thepsychologist.bps.org.uk/volume-33/september-2020/what-improv-ubuntu-and-covid-19-have-taught-me-about-leadership.

Niemiec, R. M. (2012) 'VIA character strengths: research and practice (the first 10 years)', in H. Knoop and A. Delle Fave (eds), *Well-Being and Cultures: Cross-Cultural Advancements in Positive Psychology*. Dordrecht: Springer, pp. 11–29.

Niemiec, R. M. (2020) 'Six functions of character strengths for thriving at times of adversity and opportunity: a theoretical perspective', *Applied Research in Quality of Life*, 15(2), 551–572.

Nottingham, J. (2017) *The Learning Challenge: How to Guide Your Students Through the Learning Pit to Achieve Deeper Understanding*. Thousand Oaks, CA: Corwin Press.

Obama, B. (2009) 'Remarks by the President in a National Address to America's Schoolchildren'. Speech delivered at Wakefield High School, Arlington, VA, 8 September. Available at: https://obamawhitehouse.archives.gov/the-press-office/remarks-president-a-national-address-americas-schoolchildren.

Parkinson, J. (2021) 'Matt Hancock affair: health secretary apologises for breaking social distancing guidelines', *BBC News* (25 June). Available at: https://www.bbc.co.uk/news/uk-politics-57612441.

Robinson, V. (2017) 'Capabilities required for leading improvement: challenges for researchers and developers'. Paper presented at the Australian Council for Educational Research Conference, Leadership for Improving Learning – Insights from Research, Melbourne, 28 August.

Robinson, V., Meyer, F., Le Fevre, D. and Sinnema, C. (2020) 'The quality of leaders' problem-solving conversations: truth-seeking or truth-claiming?', *Leadership and Policy in Schools*, 1–22.

Rosette, A. S., Mueller, J. S. and Lebel, R. D. (2015) 'Are male leaders penalized for seeking help? The influence of gender and asking behaviors on competence perceptions', *Leadership Quarterly*, 26(5), 749–762.

Sammons, P., Hillman, J. and Mortimore, P. (1995) *Key Characteristics of Effective Schools: A Review of School Effectiveness Research*. London: Institute of Education, University of London.

Sandberg, S. (2013) Sheryl Sandberg (MBA 1995) speaks at the Harvard Business School W50 Summit [video] (April). Available at: https://www.youtube.com/watch?v=d6xZRaITLgk.

Sankowsky, D. (1995) 'The charismatic leader as narcissist: understanding the abuse of power', *Organizational Dynamics*, 23(4), 57–71.

Schwieger, D. and Ladwig, C. (2018) 'Reaching and retaining the next generation: adapting to the expectations of Gen Z in the classroom', *Information Systems Education Journal*, 16(3), 46–54.

Scott, K. (2017) *Radical Candour: How to Get What You Want By Saying What You Mean*. London: Pan Macmillan.

Shamir, B. (2013) 'Leadership in context and context in leadership studies', in M. G. Rumsey (ed.), *The Oxford Handbook of Leadership*. New York: Oxford University Press, pp. 343–355.

Sims, S. (2017) *TALIS 2013: Working Conditions, Teacher Job Satisfaction and Retention. Statistical Working Paper* (November). Available at: https://files.eric.ed.gov/fulltext/ED604491.pdf.

Smith, A. W. (2013) *Overcoming Perfectionism: Finding the Key to Balance and Self-Acceptance.* Deerfield Beach, FL: Health Communications.

Snyder, C. R. and Lopez, S. J. (eds) (2009) *Handbook of Positive Psychology.* New York: Oxford University Press.

Staufenberg, J. (2017) 'Carter identifies 8 kinds of "decliner" and "improver" schools', *Schools Week* (17 September). Available at: https://schoolsweek.co.uk/carter-identifies-8-kinds-of-decliner-and-improver-schools.

Stoll, L., Bolam, R., McMahon, A. and Wallace, M. (2006) 'Professional learning communities: a review of the literature', *Journal of Educational Change*, 7(4), 221–258.

Taggar, S. (2002) 'Individual creativity and group ability to utilize individual creative resources: a multilevel model', *Academy of Management Journal*, 45(2), 315–330.

Vaughan, R. (2016) 'Charting the downfall of the "famous five" superheads', *TES* (14 October). Available at: https://www.tes.com/news/charting-downfall-famous-five-superheads.

Walker, A. (2006) *We Are the Ones We Have Been Waiting For: Inner Light in a Time of Darkness.* New York: New Press.

Weston, D., Hindley, B. and Cunningham, M. (2021) *Working Paper: A Culture of Improvement Reviewing the Research on Teacher Working Conditions.* London: Teacher Development Trust. Available at: https://tdtrust.org/wp-content/uploads/2021/02/A-culture-of-improvement_-reviewing-the-research-on-teacher-working-conditions-Working-Paper-v1.1.pdf.

Wheatley, M. J. (1994) *Leadership and the New Science: Learning About Organization from an Orderly Universe.* San Francisco, CA: Berrett-Koehler.

Wheatley, M. J. (2002) *Turning to One Another: Simple Conversations to Restore Hope to the Future.* San Francisco, CA: Berrett-Koehler.

Wiliam, D. (2006) 'Assessment for learning: why, what and how'. Cambridge Assessment Network seminar presented at University of Cambridge, 15 September. Available at: https://www.dylanwiliam.org/Dylan_Wiliams_website/Papers_files/Cambridge%20AfL%20keynote.doc.

Wood, A. M., Linley, P., Maltby, J., Baliousis, M. and Joseph, S. (2008) 'The authentic personality: a theoretical and empirical conceptualization and the development of the authenticity scale', *Journal of Counseling Psychology*, 55(3), 385–399.

Imperfect Leadership
A book for leaders who they don't know it all

Steve Munby
ISBN: 9781785834110

Imperfect Leadership is an honest reflection upon leadership. It is about Steve's journey, covering his highs and lows and, ultimately, how he learned to refine and improve his leadership. It is about messy, trial-and-error, butterflies-in-the-stomach leadership and about thoughtful and invitational leadership – and the positive impact it can have.

At the heart of the book are edited highlights of the twelve keynote speeches delivered to increasingly large audiences of school leaders between 2005 and 2017. These speeches, delivered at the Seizing Success and Inspiring Leadership conferences, form the structure around which Steve's story and insights are wrapped.

Steve's account covers some fundamental shifts in the English education system over this twelve-year period and describes how school leaders altered their leadership as this context changed. Furthermore, it delves into how his own leadership developed as his personal context changed, and explores how the notion that a leader needs to be good at all aspects of leadership is not only unrealistic, but is also bad for the mental and physical health of leaders – and will do nothing to attract new people into leadership positions.

Ultimately, Steve hopes that as you read this book you will see the value of imperfect leadership and of the positive impact it can make. For those reading it who have yet to step up into leadership, his sincere wish is that it will encourage and empower aspirational leaders rather than discourage them.